W9-BRZ-923

FEB 13 '91			

Twayne's English Authors Series

Sylvia E. Bowman, *Editor*

INDIANA UNIVERSITY

David Hume

 77

David Hume

By JOHN VALDIMIR PRICE

University of Edinburgh

Twayne Publishers, Inc.　::　New York

In Memoriam

F J H

Preface

This book is a general introduction to the philosopher, historian, and man of letters David Hume; it is designed primarily for the reader who knows little about Hume, something about the eighteenth century, but who is nevertheless interested in some guide to Hume's thought. In it, I have attempted to write for the novice without insulting the knowing. In doing so, I have often rephrased Hume's ideas at perhaps immoderate length; my aim, however, is exegesis and not summary. The reader who wishes a more thorough and more exacting analysis of Hume's thought can refer to the suggestions in the bibliography.

I have deliberately separated a discussion of the publication and reception of Hume's books from a discussion of the ideas found in them. As a result, the first chapter is primarily a bibliographical introduction, which gives, I hope, vital information about the intellectual climate in which Hume's writings appeared. Trying to compress a large amount of information in a necessarily short chapter is not easy, and I have often asked much of the reader's memory. The first chapter is thus an implication of what succeeding chapters contain.

The organization of the book, for the most part chronological, is deliberately unimaginative. Most modern commentaries on Hume are organized according to various large-scaled themes and ideas in his writings. In contrast, I have presented a discussion of Hume's writings in roughly the order they were published, simply because such a procedure was the most expeditious way of approaching Hume's ideas within a limited number of pages.

Throughout the book, in quoting from Hume's works and letters, I have given the source, in abbreviated form, in the text. I have followed the same practice in referring to some of the standard secondary works, such as Professor Mossner's *Life of*

David Hume. Generally speaking, I have relied upon standard editions, and I have on some occasions given cross-references to another edition of the work being quoted. The bibliography contains a complete list of the various editions quoted as well as a note about the abbreviations actually used in the text. Since the bibliography is designed to be selective and critical, I have not re-entered every item cited in the notes in order to avoid needless duplication.

For critical and helpful readings of the manuscript, I am indebted to Ernest Mossner of the University of Texas, David Norton and Richard Popkin of the University of California, La Jolla, and John MacQueen of the University of Edinburgh. Kathleen Williams of the University of California, Riverside, was kind enough to read the manuscript at a difficult time, and I am grateful for her thoroughness and good humor. I owe a particular debt of gratitude to a man I very much admire, the late Fred Hoffman, who not only read the manuscript with great care but also set an excellent example as a scholar. I have profited much from his advice and suggestions. For aid in proofreading the manuscript, I am grateful to one of my former students, Miss Ann Charters. My wife Sylvia has been more than usually helpful during each stage of the work. What more can a man ask than to have a wife who actually enjoys reading his manuscripts?

JOHN VALDIMIR PRICE

David Hume Tower
University of Edinburgh

Contents

Contents

Chronology

1711
: David Hume born April 26 (O.S.) at Edinburgh, the second son of Joseph, proprietor of Ninewells, in the parish of Chirnside, in Berwickshire.

1723–1725
: At Edinburgh College.

1725–1726
: *Treatise* "projected."

1725–1734
: Pursues education by himself at Ninewells and Edinburgh.

1726
: Leaves college.

1729–1733
: Pursues education so intently as to damage health.

1734
: Writes famous letter about health to Dr. John Arbuthnot; goes to London, then to Bristol, where he works in a merchant's office.

1734–1737
: Tours France (Paris, Reims, La Flèche). *Treatise* written mostly at La Flèche.

1737–1739
: In London, arranging for publication of *Treatise*, the first two volumes of which appear in January, 1739.

1739–1745
: In Edinburgh and Ninewells.

1740
: *Abstract of Treatise* (first two volumes) appears in March. Volume III of *Treatise* appears in November.

1741
: First volume of *Essays, Moral and Political* published.

1742
: Second volume of *Essays, Moral and Political* published.

1744–1745
: Candidate (unsuccessful) for Chair of Ethics and Pneumatical Philosophy at University of Edinburgh.

1745–1746
: Lives in London; tutor to Marquess of Annandale.

1746–1747
: London; secretary to General St. Clair.

1747
: At Cork, London, and Ninewells.

1748   *Three Essays, Moral and Political* published. *Account of Stewart* published. New edition of *Essays, Moral and Political* appears. *Philosophical Essays concerning Human Understanding* published in April. (Title changed in 1758 to *Enquiry concerning Human Understanding.*)

1749–1751   Lives in London and Ninewells.

1751–1758   In Edinburgh.

1751   Candidate (unsuccessful) for Chair of Logic at University of Glasgow. *Bellmen's Petition* published. *Enquiry concerning Principles of Morals* appears in December.

1752   *Political Discourses* published in February.

1752–1757   Keeper of Advocates' Library (now the National Library of Scotland).

1753–1756   *Essays and Treatise on Several Subjects* published, a collected, four-volume edition of Hume's works, excluding *Treatise.*

1754   *The History of Great Britain* (1603–1649) published in November.

1756   *The History of Great Britain* (1649–1689) published in November or December. (Imprint reads 1757, but volume appeared before then.)

1757   *Four Dissertations* published in February.

1758–1759   In London.

1759   *The History of England* (1485–1603), two volumes, published in March.

1759–1763   In Edinburgh, with a short visit to London in 1761.

1762   *The History of England* (55 B.C.–1485), two volumes published. First volume reviewed in December, 1761; second in February, 1762. Millar brings out "a new edition corrected" entitled *The History of England* (six volumes).

1763–1766   In London, August–October, 1763. Secretary to Lord Hertford in His Britannic Majesty's Embassy, Paris. Meets Comtesse de Boufflers in late 1763. Corresponds with Jean-Jacques Rousseau.

1766   Returns to London, bringing Rousseau with him. Quarrels with Rousseau. Publishes *Exposé succinct de la contestation . . . entre M. Hume et M. Rous-*

seau, translated later the same year as *A Concise and Genuine Account of the Dispute between Mr. Hume and Mr. Rousseau.*

1766–1767 In Edinburgh briefly.

1767–1769 In London. Under-Secretary of State, Northern Department, until January, 1768.

1769–1776 Retires to Edinburgh.

1776 Visits London and Bath. Dies at Edinburgh on August 25.

1777 Posthumous, definitive edition of *Essays and Treatises.* Autobiography, *The Life of David Hume, Esq., written by himself,* published.

1779 *Dialogues concerning Natural Religion* published, edited by his nephew, David Hume.

CHAPTER 1

Hume's Life and Publications: A Study in Controversy

B Y all accounts, the boyhood of David Hume did not suggest the subtleties and discriminations that were to become his philosophical hallmark. His autobiography, *My Own Life,* relates that he was "seized very early with a passion for Literature which has been the ruling Passion of my Life . . ."; and, in a letter written at the age of twenty-three, Hume observes "that from my earliest Infancy, I found alwise a strong Inclination to Books & Letters" (*HL,* I, 13).* He made some attempts at studying law but gave them up because of his profound interest in philosophy and literature. He matriculated at Edinburgh University in 1723 and pursued his education with no more than ordinary success. During his Edinburgh days, he wrote the earliest of his surviving literary works, a school exercise entitled "An Historical Essay on Chivalry and modern Honour." [1] His unfavorable opinion in it of the Dark Ages, typical though it was of the eighteenth century, was to alter in no important respects; in an appendix to the first volume of the *History of England,* Hume repeats substantially the same conclusions about the feudal and Anglo-Norman governments and manners that he had reached at the age of fourteen.[2]

I *Early Aspirations*

Writing a history of England, however, was not Hume's first interest, if we are to believe Hume's public and private observations about his authorship of the *Treatise of Human Nature.* In a letter of 1751 to his friend and philosophical disputant, Gilbert Elliot of Minto, Hume said the *Treatise* had been "plan'd before I was one and twenty, & compos'd before twenty five," adding that he had repented his "Haste a hundred, & a hundred times" (*HL,*

---

* *The Letters of David Hume,* ed. J. Y. T. Greig (Oxford, 1932). Standard edition of Hume's works and my code-abbreviations for them are listed in the Bibliography, *infra* pp. 167–170.

I, 158). Later, about a year after his death, the advertisement to the posthumous and authoritative edition of the *Essays and Treatises on Several Subjects* carried Hume's only public admission of his authorship of the *Treatise* as a "work which the Author had projected before he left College, and which he wrote and published not long after." And in this now-famous advertisement he publicly repudiated the *Treatise*.[3] Still, the *Treatise* contains many of Hume's most important philosophical discussions. While he altered some of his views in redacting the *Treatise* for publication in other forms, he did not indulge in a radical renunciation of his basic principles.

Hume's statement about the early, juvenilian form of the *Treatise* may be taken almost literally. While he showed no other signs of precocity, that the work could have been planned before Hume was twenty-one is not inconceivable. He led a quiet, reflective life during that period; and his thoughts were occupied with the revolutionary quality of his philosophy. Writing to his good friend Henry Home in February, 1739, Hume remarks:

Tis now a fortnight since my Book was publish'd; & besides many other considerations, I thought it wou'd contribute very much to my Tranquillity, & might spare me many Mortifications, to be in the Countrey, while the Success of the Work was doubtful. I am afraid twill remain so very long. Those, who are accustom'd to reflect on such abstract Subjects, are commonly full of Prejudices; & those, who are unprejudiz'd, are unacquainted with metaphysical Reasonings. My Principles are also so remote from all the vulgar Sentiments on this Subject, that were they to take place, they wou'd produce almost a total Alteration in Philosophy; & you know Revolutions of this kind are not easily brought about. I am young enough to see what will come of the Matter; but am apprehensive lest the chief Reward I shall have for some time will be the Pleasure of studying on such important Subjects, & the Approbation of a few Judges. (*NHL*, 3–4)

Those sanguine remarks would not cause the reader to suspect some of the difficulties Hume experienced in composing his work, the most serious of which was his health. Late in 1729, he was afflicted with poor health, probably as a result of his intense regimen of study and concentration. For about five years, this ill health continued and was the occasion of one of his most interesting letters.[4] In it, Hume gives a full description of the disorders to which both his mind and body were subject, and one of the concluding questions—"Whether I can ever hope for a Recovery?"—is almost plaintive in the suffering it reflects. Whatever the cause, Hume did recover,[5] apparently while spending three years in France, during which time the *Treatise* was actually written. Hume left for France, by way of Bristol, going first to Paris then to Rheims, and finally to La Flèche in Anjou, where he wrote most of the *Treatise*.

Only one known letter from his "retreat" at La Flèche survives, to one James Birch, whom Hume had met in Bristol in 1734, and to whom he had written a letter (*HL*, I, 22–23) from Rheims. The letter from La Flèche contains this interesting paragraph:

> As to a celebrated Professor, I do not know, if there is such to be met with at present in any part of France, especially for the Sciences, in which generally speaking the French are much inferiour to our own Countreymen. But as you know there is nothing to be learnt from a Professor, which is not to be met with in Books, & there is nothing requir'd in order to reap all possible Advantages from them, but an Order & Choice in reading them; in which besides the small Assistance I can give you, your own Judgement wou'd alone be sufficient; I see no reason why we shou'd either go to an University, more than to any other place, or ever trouble ourselves about the Learning or Capacity of the Professor.[6]

It is likely that this paragraph, from a letter written in 1735, would be more controversial in Academe today than any of the philosophical observations he was outlining in the *Treatise*.

II A Treatise of Human Nature

In spite of all his difficulties with his health and some doubts about the success of the work, Hume sold for fifty pounds the copyright for the first two volumes of the *Treatise* to John Noone, of Cheapside, on September 26, 1738; and they appeared anonymously in January, 1739. The third volume, which Francis Hutcheson, then Professor of Moral Philosophy in the University of Glasgow, read, appeared in November, 1740. Dissatisfaction, perhaps more imagined than real, with his publisher John Noone and the aid of Francis Hutcheson led Hume to find another publisher for the third volume, this time Thomas Longman; the financial arrangements are unknown. One thousand copies of each volume were printed. Hume's high hopes, expressed in letters to his friends, for the success of his three volumes were to be denied. In writing his autobiography, he remarked that the *Treatise* had fallen "*dead-born from the Press.*" [7] This statement is exaggerated but flat contradiction of it would be also. The *Treatise* did not go unnoticed; it simply was not a popular success, which is no surprise since few philosophical treatises are. Hume had said in the Advertisement to the first two volumes, "If I have the good fortune to meet with success, I shall proceed to the examination of Morals, Politics, and Criticism; which will compleat this Treatise of Human Nature. The approbation of the public I consider as the greatest reward of my labours; but am determin'd to regard its judgment, whatever it be, as my best instruction." That he clearly did not follow this intention is evidenced by the hostile reviews and the publication of the last volume twenty-one months after the first two had appeared. The interval between publication was both exciting and frustrating for Hume.

The first notice, if it could be called such, appeared on the Continent, in the *Neuen Zeitungen von gelehrten Sachen.* Containing about seven lines, the review remarked that "The author's intentions are sufficiently betrayed in the sub-title of the work, taken from Tacitus: *Rara temporum felicitas, ubi sentire, quae velis, & quae sentias, dicere, licet.*" [8] Several other articles in learned journals of the Continent called attention to the *Treatise,* but the review Hume most wanted to see appeared in the *History of the Works of the Learned.* When it appeared in two parts in the November and December issues of 1739, Hume might well have wished that the two volumes had been ignored. Without beginning "This will never do . . . ," the reviewer makes clear his opposition to Hume's ideas and methodology, as well as the claims made for the book. The first part of the review (devoted only to Book I of the *Treatise*) is heavily abusive and indulges in such comments as "this extraordinary Philosopher" and "so profound and accurate a Genius." The second part, in December, is somewhat restrained and seems to have been written by another person. The author cites Hume's abilities without sarcasm and suggests that "Time and Reason may ripen these Qualities [of 'Prudence, Tenderness, and Delicacy']" necessary to treat of human nature. Professor Mossner has conjectured that the reviewer in the November issue may have been that epitome of abuse and incompetence, the Reverend William Warburton, later bishop of Gloucester.[9] Whatever the identity of the reviewer, the reception of the *Treatise* was not what Hume wished; and he carried out a plan made prior to the review, that of publishing, in the strictest anonymity, an abstract of the *Treatise*.

Hume had thought, before the review in the *History of the Works of the Learned,* that he would send the publication an anonymous letter explaining the *Treatise*. Discretion apparently being the better part of valor, he decided to publish the abstract as a pamphlet. The *Daily Advertiser* of March 11, 1740, announced a pamphlet called *An Abstract of a late Philosophical Performance, entitled A Treatise of Human Nature, &c. Wherein the chief Argument and Design of that Book, which has met with such Opposition, and been represented in so terrifying a Light, is further illustrated and explain'd.* When the pamphlet appeared, the title was somewhat different: *An Abstract of a Book lately Published: Entituled, A Treatise of Human Nature, &c. Wherein the Chief Argument of that Book is farther Illustrated and Explained.*[10]

To me, this pamphlet represents an extraordinary effort by its author to call attention to his work. Although we might consider it a product of egotism (Hume was accused by the reviewers of having too many egotisms in his work), the *Abstract*, regarded by modern eyes, is actually designed to enforce the validity of Hume's reasonings. Other writers have sufficiently shown that Hume was not the egotistical man that he was long accused of being, and the *Abstract* is anything but vain. All of the early reviews of the first two books of the *Treatise* gave unquestionable evidence that the reviewer simply had not understood what Hume was saying. To Hume, then, it must have seemed perfectly proper to synthesize his views in an anonymous pamphlet in order to insure reviews that were at least fair. Without going into it in detail, we can observe that the *Abstract* is a lucid and cogent representation of Hume's fundamentally new ideas in the *Treatise*. Moreover, we seldom get in literature an abstract of a work by the same author; and Hume's *Abstract* strengthens our understanding of his ideas.

Unfortunately, the fate of the *Abstract* was not much better than that of the first two volumes of the *Treatise;* reviewers ignored it in passing judgment upon the *Treatise.* To expect now that Book III of the *Treatise* would meet a better fate would be almost ludicrous. Actually, its fate was worse: it attracted only one review, in the spring, 1741, issue of the French journal, published in Amsterdam, *Bibliothèque raisonée des ouvrages des savans de l'Europe.* Needless to say, it was unfavorable. Hume had tried to make the third book independent of the other two, as the Advertisement prefixed to Book III indicated. Apparently disheartened by his lack of success, he never wrote what would have been Book IV, "Of Criticism." [11]

III   Essays Moral and Political

In spite of this adversity, perhaps because of it, Hume, as he says in his autobiography, "very soon recovered the Blow, and prosecuted with great Ardour my Studies in the Country." He set to work on a group of essays called *Essays Moral and Political,* often incorrectly thought to be a recasting of the *Treatise* in more popular form. He was, in effect, not permitting his career to be circumscribed by an unfavorable reception of his first literary attempt. Thus, even as early as 1739, he was working on the *Essays Moral and Political* (1741–1742). He thought that the difficulties with the *Treatise* were more stylistic than philosophical, and he therefore devoted himself to subjects more accessible to the general reader than that of the *"experimental Method of Reasoning"* in *"MORAL SUBJECTS."* And the titles of the essays—"Of the Delicacy of Taste and passion," "Of Impudence and Modesty," "Of Simplicity and Refinement," to mention only a few—are proof of this determination to accept and to use where possible the dominant literary form of the early 1740's. The first volume of *Essays Moral and Political* appeared in late 1741, published by R. Fleming and A. Alison for Edinburgh's leading publisher, Alexander Kincaid; the second volume appeared in January, 1742, and a second edition of the first volume appeared in mid-1742.

The form into which Hume now cast some of his ideas won almost immediate acceptance by the reading public. On June 13, 1742, five months after the *Essays* had appeared, Hume wrote to his friend Henry Home, "The Essays are all sold in London; as I am inform'd by two Letters from English Gentlemen of my Acquaintance . . . I am also told that Dr [Joseph] Butler has every where recommended them." Writing his autobiography in 1776, Hume had not changed his opinion about the success of the *Essays:* "The Work was favourably received, and soon made me entirely forget my former Disappointment." These essays appeared only six years after Bishop Butler's intellectual landmark *The Analogy of Religion,* and they provided a species of reasoning that, to the modern reader, is a proper antidote to the involutions of Butler's analogical reasoning; to the eighteenth-century reader, Hume's essays must have seemed models of style and clarity after Butler's difficult prose.

The literary milieu into which Hume thrust his *Essays* was barren indeed. The great days of Swift and Pope were behind them, and both those authors were but a few years from death. Johnson's much-admired poem "London" had been published in 1738, but his *Life of Savage* was not to appear until 1744. Goldsmith was about twelve years old at the time, and he could hardly be said to be one of the leading literary figures of the 1740's. The works of James Thomson were, of course, well known to the readers of the time; but no essayist with anything to say had published anything of significance. To say that Hume's *Essays* filled a vacuum would be a gross distortion of the metaphor, but they did present "popular" essays that exhibited "close reasoning" and clarity of style. In that respect, the *Essays* of 1741–1742 were significantly different from any other essays published about that time. Thus, the stage was set for a favorable reception of Hume's writings; and it is small wonder the *Essays* met with the success the collection deserved.

One success gave hope of another, this time for the chair of Ethics and Pneumatical Philosophy at Edinburgh University, an opportunity which Hume was given in 1744. To be a philosopher is one thing; to become a professor of philosophy at a university is quite another. Hume's candidature, which his friends promoted, was objected to primarily because of heresy, real and imagined, in his writings. That the *Treatise* was not being ignored is only too evident from the ways in which it was used against Hume when he sought support for the professorship. An attack was actually mounted against Hume, and he felt obliged to defend himself in writing. Accordingly, he wrote a pamphlet in defense of himself, which he sent to Henry Home who rushed it into print, apparently without Hume's consent (*NHL*, 15). This pamphlet was advertised in the newspapers, but no copy of it was known until late 1966, when the National Library of Scotland acquired one. Entitled *A Letter from a Gentleman to His Friend in* Edinburgh: *containing Some Observations on A Specimen of the Principles concerning Religion and Morality*, said to be *maintain'd in a Book lately publish'd, intituled,* A Treatise of Human Nature, *&c.,* it was published anonymously in Edinburgh, in May, 1745 and has now been reprinted in facsimile.[12]

Unsuccessful in this attempt, Hume managed, later in 1745, to land a job of questionable value (except for a good salary)—tutor to the Marquess of Annandale, whose only drawback was a major one: he was mad as a March hare. Hume spent an unhappy year with this unfortunate young man, and then accepted a position with General James St. Clair as secretary to a proposed Canadian expedition, one which ended with an incursion into France.[13] After that, he again served General St. Clair on military embassies to Vienna and Turin.

The period of time that Hume spent with General St. Clair must be accounted as about the least interesting to anyone interested in the philosopher as man of letters, and Hume himself remarked in *My Own Life* that "These two Years were almost the only Interruptions which my Studies have received in the Course of my Life"; but he immediately added: "I passed them agreeably and in good Company." We still suspect that they were not years that afforded David Hume the kind of intellectual stimulation and camaraderie that he so much enjoyed at other periods of his life.

IV   *The Two* Enquiries *and "Of Miracles"*

In 1748, the fever of publishing returned; and Hume put out a third edition of the *Essays Moral and Political* and published what is more accurately called, though still incorrectly, a recasting of the *Treatise* than of his *Essays:* the *Philosophical Essays concerning Human Understanding* (April 25, 1748, published by Andrew Millar). By this time, Hume had achieved financial independence, and his reputation as a man of letters was shortly to be established. In 1750, he published a second edition of the *Philosophical Essays concerning Human Understanding*, as well as *An Enquiry concerning the Principles of Morals*, which restated and clarified part of Book III of the *Treatise*. Then, in 1752, he published his *Political Discourses,* containing the essays "Of Commerce," "Of Luxury," "Of Money," "Of Interest," "Of the Balance of Trade," "Of the Balance of Power," "Of Taxes," "Of Public Credit," "Of Some Remarkable Customs," "Of the Populousness of Antient Nations," "Of the Protestant Succession," and "Idea of a Perfect Commonwealth." These productive years for Hume set the pace for his literary activity for the next ten years.

In *My Own Life,* Hume remarks that the immediate reception of the *Philosophical Essays concerning Human Understanding* was not what he had wished: "On my return from Italy, I had the Mortification to find all England in a Ferment on account of Dr. Middletons Free Enquiry;[14] while my Performance was entirely overlooked and neglected." His "Performance" was not to be "overlooked and neglected" for long. For one thing, the *Philosophical Essays concerning Human Understanding* (henceforth called the first *Enquiry* since Hume later changed its title to *An Enquiry concerning Human Understanding*) contained the essay "Of Miracles," which even recently has been called, quite incorrectly, "the one thoroughly silly production of his pen."[15] Hume had omitted an early version of the essay on miracles from the *Treatise,* and he was advised by most of his friends to omit it from the first *Enquiry.*

Hume had hoped to get Bishop Butler to read his *Treatise,* and he wrote to Henry Home in December, 1737, that "Your Thoughts & mine agree with Respect to Dr Butler, & I wou'd be glad to be introduc'd to him. I am at present castrating my Work, that is, cutting off its noble Parts, that is, endeavouring it shall give as little Offence as possible . . ." (*NHL,* 2–3). Hume was, of course, referring to his discussion of miracles, which along with another essay in the first *Enquiry,* "Of a Particular Providence and of a Future State" (changed from the first edition's title "Of the Sceptical or Academical Philosophy"), attracted as much attention and refutation as the rest of his previous works combined. A helpful clue to religious thought of the mid-1750's and to Hume's reputation can be seen in an examination of some of the responses to Hume's work, particularly to "Of Miracles."

The first notice given to the essay "Of Miracles" came from an obscure Irish clergyman, the Reverend Philip Skelton, in a two-volume series of dialogues, *Ophiomaches: Or, Deism Revealed.*[16] Skelton's work is an intelligent attempt by a Christian to grapple with the problem of Deism. Cast in a series of eight dialogues, the discussions involve three Deists—Messrs. Dechaine, Templeton, and Cunningham—and one free-spoken defender of the miraculous in Christianity, the Reverend Shepherd (the names are fictitious). The treatment of Hume's "Of Miracles" is gentlemanly and scholarly, perhaps because Skelton considered Hume a Deist. In the fifth Dialogue, Shepherd answers Dechaine, who, quoting Hume's first *Enquiry*, puts forward an empirical argument against miracles. Shepherd attempts to answer Dechaine—and Hume— by combining an empirical argument with revelation:

To conclude [this argument], we cannot conceive it possible, that so many thousands of people should, in so short a time, croud into the church of *Christ*, in the teeth of all their inveterate prejudices, and of the most outrageous persecutions, had not miracles been everywhere wrought for their conviction; nor can we, without horrible blasphemy against the wisdom of God, suppose, that he should have wrought so many miracles to propagate a religion, which was to depend on the genuineness of its records, and yet not provide sufficiently, whether by Divine or human means, against the change or corruption of those records. If the ordinary methods of his providence had not been sufficient for this purpose, we cannot help concluding, that he would have vouchsafed a series of miracles, to ascertain the genuineness of the Scriptures, as well as to prove the doctrines, contained in them, to be Divine: for our conviction must have been a part of his intention, as well as that of the Christians in the Apostolic age.[17]

That Skelton's argument is tautological is easily seen, but it was a genuine attempt to establish the validity of testimony for miracles.[18]

One of the more popular books on religion in the mid-eighteenth century was John Leland's *View of the Principal Deistical Writers*.[19] Leland is openly hostile to Hume, but he attempts to be detached in his refutation. Using the convention of a letter to a friend, Leland argues that testimony is part of experience, and that Hume "cannot therefore make his argument properly bear, except he can prove, that miracles are absolutely impossible" (II, 65). Leland accuses Hume of identifying the "*miraculous nature* of an event" 'with the "*absolute impossibility* of it" (II, 65–66) and of ignoring the intervention of God in the processes of nature: "The only case therefore in which they [miracles] are never to be believed, is when they are pretended to be wrought in favour of religion" (II, 98). We should not be surprised now to learn that in his opening comments Leland is disinclined to take Hume seriously: "His writings seem, for the most part, to be calculated rather to amuse, or even confound, than to instruct and enlighten the understanding: And there are not a few things in them, that strike at the foundation of natural, as well as the proofs and evidences of revealed religion" (II, 2). Leland, like many of his contemporaries, felt that discussion or analysis of certain subjects, particularly the "truth" of religious propositions, was not to be countenanced—a view that is not uncommon today.

We would think that the maelstrom surrounding Hume's "Of Miracles" would have calmed down by 1762, especially since he had completed the six volumes of the *History of England,* which had opened new sources for his critics. On the contrary, Dr. George Campbell published in Edinburgh that year his tome *A Dissertation on Miracles: Containing an Examination of the Principles advanced by David Hume, Esq: In an Essay on Miracles;* it was probably the most comprehensive discussion of miracles to appear in the eighteenth century. Hume read the *Dissertation on Miracles* in manuscript, sent to him by his friend, the Reverend Hugh Blair. Writing to Blair in 1761, Hume states that he pursued the "ingenious performance" attentively, but perhaps without the seriousness and gravity Blair thought he should demonstrate. He observes also that the faults of the manuscript lie not so much in the composition but in the subject, and he anticipates a comment from Blair: "I know you will say, it lies in neither, but in myself alone. If that be so, I am sorry to say that I believe it is incurable" (*HL,* I, 348–49). He then offers several criticisms for the improvement of the discourse. When Campbell's work appeared on June 7, 1762, Hume wrote him a very friendly letter; and Campbell replied in kind.[20]

The Advertisement prefixed to Campbell's book is disarming:

The *Essay on Miracles* deserves to be consider'd, as one of the most dangerous attacks that have been made on our religion. The danger results not solely from the merit of THE PIECE; it results much more from that of THE AUTHOR. *The piece* itself, like every other work of Mr Hume, is ingenious; but its merit is more of the oratorial kind than of the philosophical. The merit of *the author,* I acknowledge, is great. The many useful volumes he has published of *history,* and on *criticism, politics,* and *trade,* have justly procur'd him, with all persons of taste and discernment, the highest reputation as a writer. What pity is it, that this reputation should have been sullied by attempts to undermine the foundations both of *natural religion,* and of *reveal'd!* [21]

This attitude toward Hume reflects, in general, the attitude of the Moderate clergy—men like Robert Wallace and William Robertson—and it was perhaps encouraged by Hume's unfailing good nature. Campbell's argument briefly goes like this: "Regular" miracles and "religious" ones are not the same, but both are capable of proof from testimony. Hume's whole argument is built on a false hypothesis: he incorrectly assumes that the "evidence of testimony is derived solely from experience . . ." (14). Instead, Campbell suggests, "testimony hath a natural and original influence on belief, antecedent to experience . . ." (14). He then cites some of the ways in which testimony could be advanced in favor of religion. His conclusion reminds us of Bishop Butler's method of analogical reasoning. Campbell affirms that we have no presumption against religious miracles but, in fact, experience a peculiar presumption in favor of miracles as evidence for religion. Why? Because of man's expectations of an after-life, he tends to be scrupulous in his acceptance of miracles. Thus, the evidence advanced for religious miracles is valid.

The few unhysterical responses we have briefly examined are indicative of the ambivalent attitudes that Hume's critics exhibited. Except for those who attacked him bitterly in sermons or penny pamphlets as "heretic" or "atheist," criticism of Hume's ideas was divided, as in the preceding examples, into two kinds: (1) those who apparently understood Hume but refused to take him seriously; and (2) those who understood him but were more intent upon preserving the sanctity of religion than in answering him. And even this breakdown is not so facile as it seems, for the most sympathetic readers did not always understand Hume's arguments. When they did, they frequently refused to believe that he was serious. But that Hume's first *Enquiry* had a considerable impact upon serious religious and philosophical thought is beyond question. In forming skeptical doubts about the truth-value of the a priori propositions that were the foundations for much philosophical and religious thought, Hume not only led thinkers away from the pitfalls of the unsupported generalization, but also led them into a new methodology for the exegesis of epistemological propositions. He called into question the usefulness of "testimony" as evidence in decision procedure, and he suggested the proper distinction between "faith" and "knowledge."

Amid all of this hullabaloo over Hume's "Atheism," "Deism," or whatever brand of religious heterodoxy that fitted the purposes of his antagonists, *An Enquiry concerning the Principles of Morals* appeared in December, 1751, published by Andrew Millar. Hume, writing his autobiography, said of it: "In the same Year was published at London my Enquiry concerning the Principles of Morals, which, in my own opinion (who ought not to judge on that subject) is of all my writings, historical, philosophical, or literary, incomparably the best: It came unnoticed and unobserved into the World." Again, this comment was all too often taken at face value because the second *Enquiry* went into a second edition in 1753, in the first set of Hume's collected works, *Essays and Treatises on several Subjects* (4 vols., 1753–1756).

We can understand why Hume thought the *Enquiry concerning the Principles of Morals* his best since, proportionately, he revised and reorganized it more than any of his other works. One of the reasons, perhaps the major reason, that the second *Enquiry* did not enjoy instant acclaim is attributable to the number of responses the first *Enquiry*, with "Of Miracles," was evoking. Most reviewers of the mid-eighteenth century were eager and quick to defend the sanctity of religion—natural religion, revealed religion, the Christian religion, or religion in any form. Hume's arguments in "Of Miracles" and "Of a Particular Providence and of a Future State" led most writers, to judge from the attacks on Hume, to reinstate the miraculous in religion. Not even the enlightened eighteenth century was willing to forego miracles and marvels in order to discuss or to analyze a new system of ethics. I think a conjecture that Hume's second *Enquiry* attracted only scattered attention because of the preponderant inclination of other writers to rebut his skeptical dismantling of the miraculous is not only plausible but probable.

V Political Discourses

Hume's analysis of ethics did not go totally unnoticed. It was reviewed along with his *Political Discourses,* which appeared in February, 1752, in the issue of January, 1752, of the *Monthly Review,* a periodical which began in 1749.[22] The reviewer's com-

28   DAVID HUME

ments about Hume are cordial; of the second *Enquiry,* William
Rose, the reviewer, said in his opening paragraph:

> The reputation this ingenious author has acquir'd as a fine and
> elegant writer, renders it unnecessary for us to say any thing in his
> praise. We shall only observe in general, that clearness and precision
> of ideas on abstracted and metaphysical subjects, and at the same time
> propriety, elegance and spirit, are seldom found united in any writings
> in a more eminent degree than in those of Mr. *Hume.* The work now
> before us will, as far as we are able to judge, considerably raise his
> reputation; and, being free from that sceptical turn which appears in
> his other pieces, will be more agreeable to the generality of Readers.
> His subject is important and interesting, and the manner of treating it
> easy and natural. . . .

Of the *Political Discourses,* Rose said:

> Few writers are better qualified, either to instruct or entertain their
> readers, than Mr. *Hume.* On whatever subject he employs his pen, he
> presents us with something new; nor is this his only merit, his writings
> (as we observed in the preceding article) receive a farther recom-
> mendation from that elegance and spirit which appears in them, and
> that clearness of reasoning, which distinguishes them from most others.
> The discourses now before us, are upon curious and interesting sub-
> jects; abound with solid reflections; and shew the author's great knowl-
> edge of ancient and modern history, and his comprehensive views of
> things.[23]

Like many eighteenth-century reviewers, Rose devotes almost all
of his reviews to summary and quotation; but he does use the
word "curious" several times to describe the ideas in Hume's essays. But his sympathetic attitude must have been heartening to
Hume.

Most heartening of all, apparently, was the reception of *Political Discourses:* "the only work of mine, that was successful on the
first Publication: It was well received abroad and at home," writes
Hume in *My Own Life.*[24] One of the best-known essays in this
volume, entitled "Of the Populousness of Antient Nations," involved Hume in a friendly dispute with the Reverend Robert
Wallace, with whom he exchanged many letters. Hume had read
in manuscript a composition of Wallace's entitled *A Dissertation*

on the Numbers of Mankind in Antient and Modern Times. In publishing his *Political Discourses,* Hume asked Wallace for permission to refer to his manuscript in a footnote to the essay "Of the Populousness of Antient Nations." Wallace gave the permission, and Hume's essay helped stimulate publication of Wallace's *Dissertation* in 1753. Although they disagreed, Hume helped Wallace with the redaction of his manuscript, making several suggestions for stylistic changes, particularly in the omission of Scotticisms.[25]

Hume's position, in comparison to that of Wallace, is by far the more accurate one; for Hume argues that the modern world—the eighteenth century—is more populous than antiquity. He rejects the idea of decline, so popular until the close of the seventeenth century; he rejects, with equal skepticism, the popular eighteenth-century idea of progress. Wallace, however, was supported by two members of the University of Edinburgh faculty, Kenneth Mackenzie, Professor of Civil Law, and Charles Mackie, Professor of History, certainly not the first instance in scholarship when the professors have been on the losing side. Altogether, the controversy between Hume and Wallace might serve as an example for friendly disagreement.

The *Political Discourses* introduced Hume's thought to a wider audience than he had previously enjoyed. Of the twelve discourses, eight could properly belong to the study of economics; the remainder, including the "Populousness" essay, are strictly political. Hume's approach to all of the problems presented in his discussion is always philosophical; he disregards any of the preconceived notions that might hinder him from arriving at an exact estimate, say, of the principles of public credit in "Of Public Credit." I do not mean to imply that Hume brought with him no preconceived notions at all; but he did bring to economic and political questions certain preconditions, typical of his thought, that produced lucid analyses. Those preconditions were a belief in the power of reason to settle disputes, a refusal to accept a priori conditions for matters that were strictly empirical, and an inclination to look to history for guidelines. Of at least incidental interest is the impact Hume's thought had on his friend Adam Smith, whose ideas on economics were in part anticipated by Hume.[26]

VI   The History of England

Hume was now busily engaged in several projects, including
the writing of a history of England. To John Clephane, he wrote
on January 5, 1753: "As there is no happiness without occupation,
I have begun a work which will employ me several years, and
which yields me much satisfaction. Tis a History of Britain, from
the Union of the Crowns to the present time. I have already finished the reign of King James" (*HL*, I, 170). On the importance
of history, he adds, "You know that there is no post of honour in
the English Parnassus more vacant than that of History. Style,
judgement, impartiality, care—everything is wanting to our historians; and even Rapin, during this latter period, is extremely deficient."

Hume's remark about the inadequacy of previous historians is
well taken. The reference to the history of Paul de Rapin, styled
Rapin-Thoyras (1661–1725), is a clear indication that Hume was
dissatisfied with attempts to write a history of England. Rapin, a
French Protestant, had written a history of England in French,
translated by N. Tindal in fifteen volumes, 1725–31. Other histories of England, all less distinguished than Rapin's, which appeared before Hume's include the following: Thomas Carte
(1686–1754), *A General History of England* (1747–55; 4 vols.);
Laurence Echard (1670?–1730), *The History of England, From
the First Entrance of Julius Caesar and the Romans, To the End
of the reign of King James the First* (1707, with two additional
vols. in 1718, appendix in 1720); William Guthrie (1708–1770), *A
General History of England, from the Invasion of Julius Caesar,
to the revolution in 1688* (1744–51; 4 vols.); James Ralph
(1705?–1762), *History of England during the Reigns of K. William, Q. Anne, and K. George I* (1744–46, 2 vols.); and James
Tyrrell (1642–1718), *The General History of England* (1696–
1704). If any of these works survived beyond a first edition, they
did not compete with Hume's history.

Hume's contract for the first volume of his history, devoted to
the reigns of James I and Charles I, was remarkable: he did not
have Millar publish the volume because of an astonishing offer
from the Edinburgh publishers Hamilton, Balfour, and Neill.
Gavin Hamilton offered to pay Hume twelve hundred pounds
sterling for the copyright to the first edition; he was to print two

thousand copies and no more, or so he wrote to William Strahan in 1754 (see *Life,* 302–303). Actually, the bargain finally achieved was this: Hume did not contract for more than one volume at a time, he accepted only four hundred pounds for a first edition of two thousand copies, and would entertain a proposal for six hundred pounds for a second edition (*HL,* I, 234–35, 193; cited in *Life,* 303).

The high hopes Hamilton had for the success of the volume were not vindicated when it appeared in November, 1754. Hume's disappointment is recorded in his autobiography: "I was assailed by one Cry of Reproach, Disapprobation, and even Detestation: English, Scotch, and Irish; Whig and Tory; Churchman and Sectary, Free-thinker and Religionist; Patriot and Courtier united in their Rage against the Man, who had presumed to shed a generous Tear for the Fate of Charles I, and the Earl of Strafford. . . ." The "Religionists" did indeed accuse Hume of not making the proper genuflections before the citadel of religion. The criticism was again leveled at Hume's failure to regard the church as "off limits" in controversial discussions. (See *Life,* 305–12, for a summary of some of this criticism.)

The second volume, devoted to the Commonwealth and the Restoration, dutifully appeared in late 1756 (dated 1757), and was more favorably received than its predecessor had been. Much of the initial failure of the first volume might have been attributable to Gavin Hamilton's ineptitude as a businessman, and the second volume was printed by Millar. Hume noted in his autobiography that the "Conspiracy of the Booksellers contributed very much to retard the Sale . . . ," and this charge is fairly well supported by what facts have come down to us.[27] Yet Hume was not discouraged; he renewed negotiations with Millar; and, to make a long story short, the four other volumes appeared in 1759 and 1762. They comprised a complete history of England from the invasion of Julius Caesar down to 1689.

This was the last of David Hume's major works to appear during his lifetime, and its success was such that he is still listed in the card catalogues of many libraries as "David Hume, the Historian." While the success of the *History of England* permanently removed Hume from the abyss of poverty, he enjoyed the reception of the work because of its literary merit rather than because of its financial reward. The account given by Sylas Neville in his diary,

dated May 22, 1773, is not accurate: "Baker and I supped with Dr
Home by invitation. The Dr told us a remarkable anecdote of
David Hume. When the Dr returned home in 1758 David was so
poor that he said he would give all expectations in life for £30
a year. What a change of times." [28] While Hume was not
opulent in 1758, he was not poor. Neville's account, however, does
indicate that Hume's financial success was eminently respectable
for a writer.

VII   Four Dissertations

During the time that Hume was writing the *History of England*, he also planned to publish several essays, or "dissertations,"
as he called them. These "dissertations" probably caused as much
anguish as any composition he published during his lifetime, but
their complicated publishing history need not be given in complete detail here.[29] Originally, the "four short Dissertations" were
to contain "The Natural History of Religion," "Of the Passions,"
"Of Tragedy," and one Hume designated as "some Considerations
previous, to Geometry & Natural Philosophy" (*HL*, I, 223). After
some exchange of letters, Hume and Millar planned to bring out a
volume entitled *Five Dissertations*, omitting "some Considerations
previous, to Geometry & Natural Philosophy," and adding "Of
Suicide" and "Of the Immortality of the Soul." This volume was
printed, but at Hume's request was not published. Then the "five"
were reduced again to "three," and the essays on suicide and immortality were deleted. Hume added another, "On the Standard
of Taste," and the completed work, *Four Dissertations*, appeared
on February 7, 1757. The two self-suppressed dissertations, having already been printed, did manage to get into circulation
through the offices of Millar. These two essays were published in a
pirated French translation in 1770, entitled *Two Essays;* but there
was no indication as to the identity of the author. For all the difficulty these two essays led to, they do not measure up in importance to the excellent scholarly analysis "Of the Natural History of
Religion," which, to be sure, fell into immediate opprobrium with
the religionists.

VIII   *Rousseau and Beattie*

The years from 1764 to his death in 1776 were exceedingly
pleasant for Hume, except for an attempt by certain religious

zealots to remove him from the Church of Scotland. He visited France from 1763 to 1766, serving as personal secretary for Francis Seymour Conway, earl of Hertford, who had been appointed as embassy to the Court of France. Returning to France, after a long absence, Hume had the opportunity to extend his acquaintance (by correspondence) with the Comtesse de Boufflers into intimate friendship. He thought at one time "of settling there for Life." There he met Jean-Jacques Rousseau, whom he instinctively liked; however, France was not all pleasure for him. Rousseau was never at ease with Hume, and, as a result of Rousseau's vanity and seeming paranoia, Hume was involved in an embarrassing and silly contretemps with him, when Rousseau came with Hume to England in 1766 (see *Life,* 507–32).

Although Rousseau provided Hume with no little misery during 1765–1766, Hume's last years were spent in contemplation and peace—with one other exception. James Beattie, author of *An Essay on the Nature and Immutability of Truth; in opposition to Sophistry and Scepticism* (1770), decided that Hume's writings and personality were fair game for attack, and his book made quite a reputation for him as a defender of the faith and an upholder of orthodoxy. His jeremiad against Hume can be fairly estimated in this selection from the Introduction to *An Essay on Truth:*

There is a writer now alive, of whose philosophy I have much to say. By his philosophy, I mean the sentiments he has published in a book called, A *Treatise of Human Nature,* in three volumes, printed in the year 1739; the principal and most dangerous doctrines of which he has since republished again and again. . . . I should . . . make such an encomium on the author of *the History of England* as would not offend any of his rational admirers. But why is this author's character so replete with inconsistency! why should his principles and his talents extort at once our esteem and detestation, our applause and contempt! That he, whose manners in private life are said to be so agreeable to many of his acquaintance, should yet, in the public capacity of an author, have given so much cause of just offense to all the friends of virtue and mankind. . . . That he, who succeeds so well in describing the fates of nations, should yet have failed so egregiously in explaining the operations of the mind. . . . That he, who has so impartially stated the opposite pleas and principles of our political factions, should yet have adopted the most illiberal prejudices against natural and revealed religion. . . . His philosophy has done great harm. Its admirers, I know, are very numerous; but I have not as yet met with one person, who both admired and understood it.[30]

Beattie is not clear how it is possible to admire Hume without understanding him, and we do wonder how Hume's philosophy could have done great harm if no one could understand it. We share the perplexity of Hume, who, when writing to a friend, referred to "that bigotted silly Fellow, Beattie" (*HL*, II, 301). And Beattie was not alone in attacking Hume in the philosopher's "autumnal serenity" (see *Life*, 577–88 for other attacks).

IX   Dialogues concerning Natural Religion

While the quotation from Beattie serves only as an example of the rudeness of some of Hume's disputants, its rancor was repeated after Hume's death in similar attacks, particularly upon the posthumously published *Dialogues concerning Natural Religion*. Had Hume been able to publish this work during his lifetime, it would undoubtedly have inspired replies which would have made all previous accounts of Hume's religious infidelity seem like panegyrics in comparison. In fact, the *Dialogues* raised very few hostilities, presumably because a dead man is not much of a threat to an Established Order in religion.

The *Dialogues* was composed between 1751 and 1755; the first mention of it appears in a letter of March 10, 1751, to Sir Gilbert Elliot, who was asked to make some suggestions for the arguments of one of the speakers, Cleanthes, the empirical theist (see *HL*, I, 153–57). Too, it is probable that Hume was working on the *Dialogues* at the same time he wrote his "Natural History of Religion." When Hume had asked Elliot, among others, including Adam Smith, about the advisability of publishing the *Dialogues*, he was strenuously advised not to do so. In a letter of October 6, 1763, Hume ironically threatened to dedicate the *Dialogues* to the Reverend Hugh Blair, another friend who read the manuscript: "I have no present thoughts of publishing the work you mention: but when I do, I hope you have no objection of my dedicating it to you" (*NHL*, 72).

Blair had said of the work, in a context mentioning Hume's relations with the *philosophes* of Paris, "But had you gone one step farther—I am well informed, in several Poker Clubs in Paris your Statue would have been erected. If you will show them the MSS of certain Dialogues perhaps that honour may still be done you. But for Gods sake let that be a posthumous work, if ever it shall see the light: Tho' I think it had better not." [31] In spite of this opposition—or perhaps because of it—Hume undertook some elaborate measures to insure at least the posthumous publication of the *Dialogues*. In a letter of June 8, 1776, to his publisher William Strahan, Hume wanted to have five hundred copies of the *Dialogues* printed when he returned to Edinburgh; and he would have given the "literary Property of the whole" to Strahan to use as he wished after these copies were printed (see *HL*, II, 323–24).

The increasing decline of his health mitigated against publication during his life; and in a codicil to his will, dated August 7, 1776, he revoked a passage in his will authorizing Adam Smith to publish the *Dialogues*. In his will, Hume had left all of his manuscripts to Smith, "Desiring him to publish my Dialogues concerning Natural Religion. . . ." In the codicil, he left his manuscript first to Strahan to publish, stating that, if the *Dialogues* was not published within two and a half years after his death, it was to be published by his nephew, also named David Hume. Hume left two, possibly three, copies of the manuscript; and he gave one to Smith in case an accident should prevent either Strahan or his nephew from publishing the work. As it happened, William Strahan apparently permitted young David, who was only nineteen when his uncle died, to publish the *Dialogues;* the book appeared in late 1779, without any editorial apparatus or even so much as the publisher's name, though contemporary notices give Robinson of London as the bookseller. The *Dialogues* was advertised in the *Weekly Magazine*, Edinburgh, October, 1779, and also in the *Monthly Review*, London, December, 1779 (see *Dialogues*, 96). A French edition appeared in the same year and a German one in 1781. The *Dialogues* apparently sold well in Britain because a second edition appeared also in 1779.

The *Dialogues concerning Natural Religion* was accorded at least two extensive notices in Great Britain, the first being that of Thomas Hayter, *Remarks on Mr. Hume's Dialogues, concerning Natural Religion,* published in 1780. The pamphlet, sixty-five pages long, is devoted exclusively to a consideration of the *Dialogues*. Hayter, the title-page informs us, was a "Fellow of King's College, Cambridge; and one of the Preachers at his Majesty's Chapel in Whitehall." Hayter has the distinction of being one of

the very few prior to the twentieth century who was not fooled by
Hume's pious disclaimers and by the ostensible victory of Cleanthes over Philo in the work. While innumerable commentators
have tried to vindicate Hume's irreligion and to drag him in as a
true brother of the church,[32] Hayter recognized Humean thought
when he read it: "Let us consider however that Mr. HUME, after
the great nominal superiority attributed to CLEANTHES, could not
possibly, without appearance of vanity, have appointed CLEAN-
THES his representative. The fact indeed indisputably is, that
PHILO, not CLEANTHES, personates Mr. HUME." [33]

Hayter's analysis of Hume is a familiar kind: with people like
Hume for its "friends," religion needs no enemies. He is scrupu-
lously fair to Hume, but he understands fully neither Hume's
method nor his principles. Philo's theological mistakes are the result, Hayter argues, of his lack of familiarity with the truth of the
gospels. Like many eighteenth-century commentators Hayter
identified religion with Christianity, in the manner of Fielding's
Thwackum in *Tom Jones:* "When I mention religion, I mean the
Christian religion; and not only the Christian religion, but the
Protestant religion; and not only the Protestant religion, but the
Church of England." Hume was challenging, not only the conclusions drawn from age-old precepts, but the validity of those precepts as well; and this intent Hayter failed to see.

Hayter is clever in his answer to Hume; for, where possible, he
uses Hume's own texts against him; and he "reads" the texts
closely. He quotes from Hume frequently (about one-fourth of
the pamphlet is quotation) and tries to demonstrate logical errors
in Hume's thought. Quoting from the second edition, Hayter says:

PHILO . . . maintains religion to be the parent of evil, rather than of
good: more a friend to vice, than virtue—The instance of the bad
tendency of religion, produced by PHILO at p. 249, carries a very
striking peculiar air. "Many religious exercises are entered into with
seeming fervour, where the heart at the time, feels cold and languid:
a habit of dissimulation is by degrees contracted: and fraud and
falshood become the predominant principle." Concise piece of demonstration! A man performs certain religious offices negligently—is
rendered by that means a hypocrite—quickly after a complete rogue!
when such unbounded licentiousness of inference is freely and un-
blushingly practised, there seems to be no reason why one man, as
well as another, may not presume to draw conclusions.[34]

It is likely that Hume, in the passage Hayter quotes, is remarking upon some of the social necessities of piety; but Hayter has cogently suggested that the activities Philo mentions do not necessarily follow one from another. In context, however, Hume seems to refer to a psychological, not a logical, progression. Still, Hayter's answer is better than the name-calling of others.

The second reply to Hume's *Dialogues* appeared in 1781 in Joseph Milner's *Gibbon's Account of Christianity considered: Together with some Strictures on Hume's Dialogues concerning Natural Religion.* Milner was, the title-page tells us, "Master of the Grammar-School of Kingston upon Hull." Considerably more zealous in his promotion of Christianity than Hayter, Milner employs a method simple to the point of being narrow-minded: "I speak seriously, I never knew a man who gave probable evidence of an honest, careful, insight into himself, and of a just cultivation of all proper means of informing himself concerning God, his duty and the value of his soul, and the evidences of Christianity, but he would ingenuously confess he was thus corrupt and sinful: And, as far as I can judge from observation, the direct contrary was the case of all who were of a different opinion" (104). In other words, neither Hume nor Gibbon gave a careful, serious consideration to the evidence of Christianity; if they had, they could not have failed to be aware of their corruption and sinfulness, as well as of the truth of Christianity. In fact, Milner verges several times upon an identification of Christianity with an awareness of one's own personal sinfulness.

Now that Milner has established Hume's gross inattention to the evidence of salvation, etc., he is in a position to introduce the ad hominem argument. Quoting Hume's view of a future state, as expressed in the *Dialogues*, Milner observes that "The tendency of these passages is still more poisonous, to teach us that what Christianity offers in a future life is not worth the having, and that the belief of it is an enemy to all true virtue in this" (120). Milner continues, occasionally breaking into apostrophes to the "force of Scripture-truth," his denigration of both Hume and Gibbon for their failure to accept the validity of the gospels when it was so easily done. All of Hume's suggestions or observations are challenged on the grounds of being either inimical to Christianity or violations of divine law because Hume thinks the way he does. Like Hayter, Milner was not fooled by the declaration in favor of

Cleanthes that closes the *Dialogues:* ". . . it is evident from the whole tenour of the book, and still more so from the entire scepticism of his former publications, that Philois [*sic*] is his favourite. Sincerity constitutes no part of a philosopher's virtue" (199). Milner finally concludes that Hume is beyond the reach of salvation (although Gibbon is not), and he implies that he will be severely dealt with on Judgment Day.

Posthumous controversy over Hume's irreligion or skepticism was often vitriolic, and the publications of the *Dialogues concerning Natural Religion* may have sparked some of the denunciations of Hume. Had the philosopher lived longer, he probably would have been less perturbed by the attacks than his attackers were at his seeming indifference to their extravagances and to their alleged concern for his soul.[35]

When David Hume died on August 25, 1776, Adam Smith said of his life and death, in a famous letter:

Thus died our most excellent, and never-to-be-forgotten friend; concerning whose philosophical opinions men will no doubt judge variously, every one approving or condemning them as they happen to coincide, or disagree with his own; but concerning whose character and conduct there can scarce be a difference of opinion. His temper, indeed, seemed to be more happily balanced, if I may be allowed such an expression, than that perhaps of any other man I have ever known. . . . The extreme gentleness of his nature never weakened either the firmness of his mind, or the steadiness of his resolutions. . . . Upon the whole, I have always considered him, both in his lifetime, and since his death, as approaching as nearly to the idea of a perfectly wise and virtuous man, as perhaps the nature of human frailty will admit. (Reprinted in *HL*, II, 452)

CHAPTER 2

Youth and Energy:
The Remembered Treatise

I Major Ideas in the Treatise

A TREATISE *of Human Nature: Being an Attempt to introduce the experimental Method of Reasoning into MORAL
SUBJECTS* is in many ways a conventional dissertation in philosophy. For example, the first book, *Of the Understanding,* seems to
be an exposition along the same lines as John Locke's *Essay concerning Human Understanding,* and Hume treats the same subjects as Locke. Despite the emphasis on Newtonian reasoning in
both Hume and Locke, Hume's *Treatise* in no way ignores the
traditional problems of philosophy. Yet in a century more appre-
ciative of Hume than the nineteenth, one commentator has said,
and many have agreed, about the *Treatise* that "His work is, and
will remain, the inevitable starting-point for all further investiga-
tion of these subjects ['Necessary Connection' and the 'Problem of
Induction']." [1]

Unfortunately, we know little about the composition of the
Treatise, although an interesting letter to Michael Ramsay has recently come to light in, of all places, the Czartoryski Museum in
Cracow, Poland. Hume recommends that his friend read certain
works of Nicolas Malebranche, George Berkeley, and Pierre
Bayle, in order that he may read the manuscript of Hume's
Treatise with greater profit and make, Hume hopes, useful criticisms. He also mentions Michael's cousin, Andrew Michael Ramsay, better known as the Chevalier Ramsay. The Chevalier Ramsay had extended many kindnesses to Hume, but Hume's low
opinion of his philosophical abilities made him reluctant to let the
Chevalier read his *Treatise:* "I shall be oblig'd to put all my Papers into the Chevalier Ramsay's hands when I come to Paris;
which I am really sorry for. For tho' he be Freethinker enough not

to be shockt with my Liberty, yet he is so wielded to whymsical
Systems, & is so little of a Philosopher, that I expect nothing but
Cavilling from him. I even fortify myself against his Disapprobation & am resolv'd not to be in the least discouraged by it,
if I should chance to meet with it." [2] This letter, written August
31, 1737, indicates that the principles of the *Treatise* were almost
completely formed and that Hume was ready to present his philosophy to the world.

In the Introduction to the *Treatise*, Hume disavows the "te-
dious lingering method" of past thinkers as likely not to lead to a
comprehension of human nature; and, in a curious metaphor, he
likens human nature to a citadel whose outskirts have occasionally
been ambushed or captured but whose center has never been
taken. The problem of the philosopher using the "experimental
Method of Reasoning" is to master human nature, freely confessing whatever ignorance may remain.

Writing "Of the Origin of our Ideas," Hume divides all perceptions of the mind into ideas and impressions; the latter group includes the impressions of sensation—of the special bodily senses—
and the impressions of reflection, the passions, desires, and emotions.[3] These perceptions, and their assuming forms, are further
divided into simple and complex; and Hume gives to the term
"idea" a broader range of meaning than it has in Locke since it
includes concepts, notions, fancies, conjectures, and so forth. We
repeat impressions in the memory, where an impression is recollected with most of its original force, or in the imagination, where
an impression is recollected with little of its original force, "a perfect idea." The imagination has the ability to synthesize and re-
combine all the ideas at its command.

We might be tempted to think that this distinction between
"impressions" and "ideas" was simply a repetition of Locke's view
and Berkeley's additions.[4] On the contrary, Hume's *Treatise* is
more a criticism of Locke and Berkeley than a supplement to
them. This distinction Hume counts as his "first principle" and will
admit nothing into the contents of the mind except impressions
and ideas. Hume's epistemology also gives impressions precedence over ideas, so that impressions actually create ideas. When
an idea is ambiguous, a person may seek the impression which
was the occasion of it. Finding no impression for the "idea," one
can conclude "that the term is altogether insignificant" (*Abstract*,

11). Hume uses his distinction between ideas and impressions as an empirical check against what he considers a widespread tendency to discourse on ideas not occasioned by an impression or collection of impressions.

This simple but subtle arrangement of the activity of the understanding leads Hume, by equally simple logic, into some startling pronouncements about cause and effect. When Locke noted in his discussion "Of the Association of Ideas" in the *Essay concerning Human Understanding,* that ideas not allied by nature could combine because of custom, he also took notice of the peculiar associations of ideas which sometimes arise, only to suggest the damaging moral or emotional effects such associations could have. Hume writes of the "kind of Attraction" that certain ideas have for each other, but he suggests that the causes of this attraction are unknown "and must be resolv'd into *original* qualities of human nature . . ." (*Treatise,* I, i, 4; 13). Hume's definition of certain traditional philosophical terms now becomes more subjective than philosophers like Descartes would have wished; substance, for example, is defined as nothing more than a "collection of simple ideas" united by the imagination and associated with specific phenomena. The suggestiveness of complex ideas becomes so great, Hume says, that we create associations that have no corollaries in nature. After much preliminary analysis of our ideas of space and time, of cause and of knowledge and probability, Hume affirms that subjective, individually-experienced custom is the unifying power or agent between cause and effect, that the contiguity and the constant conjunction of two events impose upon our minds so strong a sense of permanent relation that we cannot disassociate them.

This mind-imposed relationship between two events is a product of experience. We experience X prior to and contiguous to Y, and we infer that X causes Y; Hume states that this inference can never amount to a demonstration—that is, a proof of which an antithesis cannot, given the rules of logic, be imagined, e.g., that $2 + 2 = 5$. Experience teaches us to reason from cause to effect, because we assume that the unity of nature's laws will persevere; from these two observations we always conclude that "like causes, in like circumstances, will always produce like effects" (*Abstract,* 15). Since we can never know exactly if the future will be conformable to the past, or if events will always "behave" the same

way, we must recognize that custom, not reason, is the guide of
life. All knowledge must then be probable, unless it is tautological; neither custom nor pure reason can lead to acquisition of immutable knowledge; and knowledge which passes itself off as immutable is, at the very least, suspect.

This position with regard to the possibility of human knowledge is likely to produce skepticism, and Hume is concerned to
analyze the "sceptical and other systems of philosophy" (*Treatise*,
I, iv, 1; 180). The classical statement on skepticism belongs to the
Hellenistic skeptic, Sextus Empiricus, to whom Hume actually refers in the *Enquiry concerning the Principles of Morals*. In addition, he probably derived knowledge of Pyrrhonian skepticism
from Pierre Bayle's *Dictionnaire Historique* or from Montaigne's
Apologie pour Raimond Sebond.[5] Briefly, Hume credits Pyrrhonism with a dogmatic assumption that all questions concerning
matters of probability are uncertain, and that certainty is not to
be found in the world.

In discussing Pyrrhonian skepticism[6] in the *Treatise*, as well as
in later works, Hume maintained that the Pyrrhonian position was
logically irrefutable but psychologically untenable; the distractions
of human nature subdue extreme skepticism: "I may, nay I must
yield to the *current of nature*, in submitting to my senses and understanding; and in this blind submission I shew most perfectly
my sceptical disposition and principles. . . . If we believe, that
fire warms, or water refreshes, 'tis only because it costs us too
much pains to think otherwise" (*Treatise*, I, iv, 7; 269–70 [my
italics]).[7] In other words, we cannot resist the impingement of
recurring events upon our minds. Reason is not a guide to life, but
neither is unmitigated skepticism. The true philosopher must be
skeptical of propositions advanced as certainties, but he must also
be ironically aware of the logical disproportions between philosophy and living.

Hume has also raised the problem of inductive reasoning in the
first volume of the *Treatise*: he would take literally Pope's line in
the *Essay on Man*, "What can we reason, but from what we
know?" (I, 18). Knowledge for Hume depends upon two activities of the mind: the impingement of simple impressions upon the
senses, and the causal ordering of ideas corresponding to those
impressions. Thus, the mind creates a series of inferences which it
accepts as true, but which at any moment could be falsified. In a

rather loose sense, Hume is applying the *post hoc ergo propter hoc* principle of logic to the experience of the human being in a series of events. We may indeed see X precede Y on any number of occasions, but we cannot say that reason teaches us that X causes Y. While we can be relatively sure that the sun will rise every morning, as it has in the past, we express only a probability, not a fact. The ultimate problem lies in constructing for all events a probability calculus that will tell us specifically what our margin of error can be.

Closely associated with the problem of induction and causality is Hume's philosophy of belief, which he equates with opinion and defines as "A LIVELY IDEA RELATED TO OR ASSOCIATED WITH A PRESENT IMPRESSION" (*Treatise*, I, iii, 7; 96). This definition emphasizes the way a mind "feels" (Hume's word) about an idea to which it has given assent; as a belief, it is recollected with a much stronger force or vivacity than is an idea to which we have not given assent. For example, we believe that the sun will rise in the morning. The vivacity of that idea is much stronger than a feeling that the sun *won't* rise in the morning; the former idea is, therefore, more active and forceful in our minds than the latter; hence, we act as if it were true. In an appendix to this section, Hume admits that it is impossible to explain perfectly the feeling or "manner of conception," but he describes the function of a belief: it is different from a fictitious idea, not in its organization, structure, or essence, but in the *manner* it is conceived. To continue with the preceding example, the manner in which we conceive a belief that the sun will rise tomorrow is more intense than the manner in which we might conceive that the sun will not rise tomorrow. When analyzing any event, we must not begin by believing that it has a cause, but should seek to discover what events, if any, are related to it and in what way they induce us to believe in causality.

Hume's efforts to clarify the meaning of such concepts as "causality" may seem trivial to the twentieth century and obvious to anyone. Yet Hume raised valuable doubts about a priori assumptions in philosophy and in natural science. By showing that the imputation of certainty to a particular event was a product of mental, not physical, operations, he at least suggested a new method for solving some of the traditional problems of philosophy; or he suggested that the problems could not be formulated in language accurate enough to contain the possibility of their answer. Until mankind achieved a method of discourse suitable for the solution of problems unsolvable in traditional philosophical discourse, it would have to abandon dispute over these problems or risk indulging in pointless subtleties.

Although the method was new, the results were not always so cogent as Hume could have wished. I have hitherto neglected to mention the concept of "self" as it appears in Book I of the *Treatise*, mainly because of widespread disagreement, including some apparent contradictions in Hume's own words, about selfhood in Humean philosophy.[8] These difficulties in conceptualizing self occur in the discussion "Of personal identity" in Book I: other selves "are nothing but a bundle or collection of different perceptions, which succeed each other with an inconceivable rapidity, and are in a perpetual flux and movement" (*Treatise*, I, iv, 6; 252). Yet, prior to that definition, Hume had said that to have a concept of self, one would have had to experience an impression which gave rise to the concept of self; and that impression would have to be unchanging and constant. But we have no such impression, only a succession of various passions and sensations, from which it is impossible to derive a specific impression of self: "consequently there is no such idea" (*Treatise*, I, iv, 6; 252). While Hume distinguishes between two sorts of "personal identity," he considers memory the source of personal identity. Since memory is faulty, we cannot extend our concept of self beyond it; and Hume suggests that disputes about self are more verbal than philosophical.[9]

The ambiguity shrouding any concept of self does not prevent Hume from analyzing the "Passions" in Book II of the *Treatise* in terms of their effect upon self. The self is the object of thoughts of pride and humility; the self is not the cause of such passions, by which Hume means bodily appetites, such as pride and humility. Pride and humility, to continue Hume's example, arise in the mind when it is presented with the idea of their cause—beauty, strength, agility, wit, etc.; for that matter, almost any stimuli could give rise to pride or humility or to any other passion. The association of ideas in the mind leads to an identification of the alleged cause of the passion with the object. Hume applies the theory of Book I to this misconception and asserts that the causes of pride and humility are *natural* but not *original*: "'tis utterly impossible they shou'd each of them be adapted to these passions

by a particular provision, and primary constitution of nature"
(*Treatise*, II, i, 3; 281). The same argument is applied to the passions of love and hatred.

In general, much of Book II is not really a supplement to Book
I of the *Treatise*, and its digressions are more interesting than
illuminating. Hume discusses the four passions of pride and humility, love and hatred, to indicate that the laws of association are
as important in mental operations as the law of gravity is in
physics; in this way, the argument of Book II is connected with
Book I.[10] In spite of its defects, and sometimes its seemingly
pointless forays into eighteenth-century psychology, Book II is a
preparation for the moral theory of Book III.[11]

The passions are first divided into *primary* and *secondary*. Primary passions are instinctive, arising without any antecedent perception "from the constitution of the body, from the animal spirits
[lust or hunger], or from the application of objects to the external
organs" (*Treatise*, II, i, 1; 275). Secondary passions are the result
of prior impressions of pleasure or pain, and these passions are
further subdivided into direct and indirect ones. Direct secondary
passions include those violent passions—"desire, aversion, grief,
joy, hope, fear, despair and security" (*Treatise*, II, i, 1; 277)—and
the calm passions, which proceed from the contemplation of
things external to us.[12] The indirect secondary passions are the
result of prior impressions of pleasure or pain while mixed with
other qualities—"pride, humility, ambition, vanity, love, hatred,
envy, pity, malice, generosity . . ." (*Treatise*, II, i, 1; 276–77).

Hume admits that these divisions are "vulgar and specious,"
and he uses them solely for convenience, in order to clarify the
affectiveness of ideas when related by something to oneself. The
separate passions, as well as ideas, can have no effect on one another unless the mind imposes upon them a relation that creates
either pain or pleasure. Hume is thus asserting the subjective
affectiveness of passions upon individual human beings and explaining why X leads to pleasure in Mr. Jones and to pain in Mr.
Smith. As is clear, this classification of the passions strengthens his
argument for the mind's function in imposing causal relationships
upon various events.

Hume fortifies his attack upon the metaphysical bugbears of
ethics in Part III of Book II, "Of the Will and Direct Passions," by
applying his same method: the uncertainty of causality. The con-

stant conjunction of two or more events and an *ipse dixit* moral judgment about them is inadmissible in Humean epistemology and in Humean ethics. In discussing the will, Hume argues that reason *by itself* never leads the will to any action, and that reason cannot successfully overcome the passions in an action of the will. The point is neatly stated in a famous piece of Humean rhetoric: "Reason is, and ought only to be the slave of the passions, and can never pretend to any other office than to serve and obey them" (*Treatise*, II, iii, 3; 415). Reason influences our conduct in only two ways: by directing the attention of a passion to that which is a proper object of the passions, or by discovering connections between events so as to give rise to a passion. Reason is, in other words, not capable of assessing the events and actions that contribute to the distinction between good and evil.

That premise is the starting-point for Hume's analysis "Of Morals" in Book III of the *Treatise*, although he does feel that contemplation has some role in the moral approval or disapproval an individual may make of certain situations. Moral distinctions for Hume arise only from a "moral sense." [13] Vice and virtue are not discoverable by reason, and Hume makes feelings rather than judgments the substance of morality. Good and evil express themselves in terms of particular pleasures and pains, and no absolute rules of right and wrong can be invoked to explain morality.

In this approach, Hume has deviated from many of the traditional notions of morality. One form of ethics has always assumed that man was capable of knowing his duty, of being able to distinguish between right and wrong, and of making the correct moral choice when confronted with events demanding judgment. Knowledge of moral duty was assumed to be on a par with knowledge of fact. Another form of ethics suggested that knowledge could influence behavior in some way, however small. Hume has rejected both of these views by arguing that knowledge cannot be a motive in the execution of moral "duties." [14] In fact, Hume seemingly rejects the concept of moral duty altogether, emphasizing instead the role of desires and beliefs. Desire, which Hume does not equate with desire for pleasure, is the basis for personal behavior and action; and beliefs have very little effect on these desires, except to indicate a method by which certain desires can be realized.

The source of moral judgments and moral inclinations lies in the peculiar constitution of man. Hume invokes a doctrine based on *sympathy* in order to explain why certain acts give us pleasure, while others give us pain. When we see an act that improves the general welfare of mankind, it evokes a favorable response in us. Sentiments, either of favor or disgust, evolve from the contemplation of events or people and from the way they affect our sympathies. When an act or event or person calls forth in us a sentiment of moral approval, we call it "virtuous." Consequently, moral rules should not be oppressively absolute, and morality is really, for Hume, a matter of taste—as is beauty or a sense of humor. Hume has also given short shrift to the method of some rationalists who derive the imperative *ought* from a simple infinitive. In other words, Hume cannot see and will not accept the allegedly logical progression from an assertion ("To love one's neighbor is good.") to the moral imperative ("Love thy neighbor!").

II *Hume's Imagery in the* Treatise

Very little is made of the use of images—metaphors, similes, analogies—in philosophic discourse, perhaps because philosophers like to think of imagery as belonging to "poetic" discourse and not to the "serious" business of philosophy. T. H. Green, who takes only brief notice of Locke's metaphor of impression in his introduction to Hume's *Treatise*, otherwise ignores Hume's imagery (*Works*, I, 9). Writing about the reception of ideas in the understanding, Locke says, "These simple ideas, when offered to the mind, the understanding can no more refuse to have, nor alter when they are imprinted, nor blot them out. . . ." [15] The metaphor of impression in Hume's *Treatise* describes perceptions which enter into our consciousness with the most "force and violence." The term suggests a perception that is indelible and irreducible; it cannot be divided into smaller components, and it enjoys something of the stability of the printed word.

Yet this metaphor is not always consistent because Hume describes the mind as a "heap or collection of different perceptions" (*Treatise*, I, iv, 2; 207). Impressions or perceptions do not enter the mind in orderly coherence, and that is why the "heap" metaphor is informative. The mind must take this heap of impressions, as a printer might take a bundle of printed but unsorted sheets, and organize them coherently; the means by which the mind organizes these impressions is, of course, experience. The metaphor of impression is further qualified when Hume describes impressions as "internal and perishing existences" (*Treatise*, I, iv, 2; 194). The memory apparently can recall impressions from the "heap," but others are doomed to "perish" without supplying ideas to the mind. Hume attributes to actions the same perishable quality that he finds in impressions: "Actions are by their very nature temporary and perishing . . ." (*Treatise*, II, iii, 2; 411).

Hume has described the mind as a "heap or collection of different perceptions," yet he does not lack for other metaphors for describing the mind. In a section entitled "Of the Love of Fame," Hume writes of the "fabric of the mind, as with that of the body," comparing the similarities in several minds to the similarities in bodies (*Treatise*, II, i, 11; 318). Minds, to continue Hume's metaphor, are all woven the same way; and the inquirer into human nature can assume a similarity of structure, thought processes, and responses. The "fabric" metaphor defines in some way the structure of the mind: "In general we may remark, that the minds of men are *mirrors* to one another, not only because they *reflect* each others emotions, but also because those *rays of passions*, sentiments and opinions may be often *reverberated*, and may *decay away* by insensible degrees. Thus the pleasure, which a rich man receives from his possessions, being thrown upon the beholder, causes a pleasure and esteem . . . and being once more *reflected*, become a new *foundation* for pleasure and esteem in the beholder" (*Treatise*, II, ii, 5; 365 [italics mine]). Untangling this mixed metaphor, we discover that Hume regards other minds as capable of generating sympathetic passions. The metaphor also postulates a similarity between the methods by which separate minds adapt themselves to the expressions of other minds. Or the passions may simply cancel each other out and slowly diminish.

A mirror image has been common enough in English literature for conveying ideas about esthetics, ethics, and politics. Hume, like all philosophers faced with the difficulty of conceptualizing mind for their readers, tries whatever seems feasible. The following analogy is, however, more subtle than preceding ones: "Now if we consider the human mind, we shall find, that with regard to the passions, 'tis not of the nature of a wind-instrument of music, which in running over all the notes immediately loses the sound after the breath ceases; but rather resembles a string-instrument, where after each stroke the vibrations still retain some sound, which gradually and insensibly decays" (*Treatise,* II, iii, 9; 440–41). Hume is at least consistent in mixing his metaphors. The passions, being "slow and restive," will not be produced distinctly but will be mixed with other, if fainter, passions. A passion, apparently, cannot be, in Locke's words, a "clear and distinct" perception; nor can it exist without being related to some other passion. This relationship is perhaps appreciated more clearly in a metaphor Hume used earlier, in which he presented the four passions of pride and humility, love and hatred in a square as follows (see *Treatise,* II, ii, 2; 333):

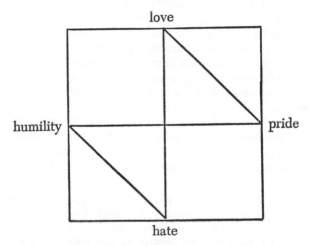

In Hume's moral philosophy and in his discussion of certain basic emotions, his metaphors clearly indicate that no emotion or passion can be experienced or conceived as a distinct entity in the mind. The indistinctness of passions suggests that confusion can easily be the governing principle of a mind incapable of distinguishing anger from hatred or fear from despair.

The preceding metaphors are all used to conceptualize mind as it expresses or experiences passions. In the first book of the *Treatise,* Hume, in describing his theory of knowledge, employs one of his best-known metaphors: "The mind is a kind of theatre, where several perceptions successively make their appearance; pass, repass, glide away, and mingle in an infinite variety of postures and situations." Thinking that this metaphor might be misleading,

Hume soon adds that "The comparison of the theatre must not mislead us. They are successive perceptions only, that constitute the mind; nor have we the most distant notion of the place, where these scenes are represented, or of the materials, of which it is compos'd" (*Treatise*, I, iv, 6; 253).

These words represent Hume's allegedly atomistic conception of the mind but are certainly at variance with the earlier description of the mind as a "heap" of perceptions. However, I think Hume is trying to indicate the manifold ways in which impressions and ideas can make their way into the mind; and, if he uses different metaphors, he is attempting to prevent us from confusing the function of the mind with its structure. Of the latter, it seems, we can have little knowledge but must be content with knowing the way the mind operates. The mind is unable to reject those things in the external world which present themselves to the mind through the senses: it may not acknowledge their force, and they may not convince; but, so long as the senses are active, the mind cannot prevent perceptual activity.

Perhaps the best metaphor, and the most complicated, that Hume uses to define mind occurs shortly after the "theatre" metaphor. Using the word "soul" as a synonym for mind, a frequent eighteenth-century practice, Hume says:

> In this respect, I cannot compare the soul more properly to any thing than to a republic or commonwealth, in which the several members are united by the reciprocal ties of government and subordination, and give rise to other persons, who propagate the same republic in the incessant changes of its parts. And as the same individual republic may not only change its members, but also its laws and constitutions; in like manner the same person may vary his character and disposition, as well as his impressions and ideas, without losing his identity. (*Treatise*, I, iv, 6; 261)

The intent of this analogy is clear. This conception of mind is not atomistic, but sees the mind as a progression of events and things that supplement, shape, and redefine themselves, as well as future events. The mind becomes a process and is not like a book, or Locke's blank slate, or any fixed entity. If I may extend Hume's metaphor, we can think of the mind as undergoing evolution and development, just as the political state does. Unless subjected to violent revolutions, it always contains something of the same structure and function it had when first formed. In other words, the ways in which the mind operates remain, for the most part, the same—as do the operations of the state. The function of either is an indication of its structure; but, unlike physical structures, either is involved in continual process and change.

If the mind is a collection of various perceptions, something must occur to give certitude to some of these. They must be organized in some way to contribute to our understanding of events. In order to illustrate the connections between events or facts, Hume relies upon an eighteenth-century commonplace: the metaphor of the chain.[16] In analyzing the "component parts of our reasonings concerning cause and effect," Hume speaks of the "chain of argument or connexion of causes and effects" involved in our acceptance of the fact of Caesar's murder on the Ides of March (*Treatise*, I, iii, 4; 83). Without the authority of memory or sense-perception, our acceptance of the testimony of historians as fact would be unfounded: "Every link of the chain wou'd in that case hang upon another; but there wou'd not be any thing fix'd to one end of it, capable of sustaining the whole . . ." (*ibid.*). A chain of argument used to support any fact must be linked to something substantial and verifiable.

The same point arises later in Hume's discussion "Of unphilosophical probability," where he remarks that we can have no assurance of any point of ancient history without accepting the validity of an immeasurable "chain of arguments." Hume then points out that an argument has been raised against Christianity by supposing "each link of the chain in human testimony" capable only of probability and "liable to a degree of doubt and uncertainty" (*Treatise*, I, iii, 8; 145). For strategic reasons—since Hume is not defending the evidence of Christianity, but historical evidence—Hume finds fault with this argument. He does, however, explain how the mind manages to preserve, despite good reasons to do otherwise, some belief in events long past; the mind retains a "feeling" of probability when, strictly speaking, probabilities should be reduced to nil.

The "links are innumerable" in connecting "an original fact with the present impression," but we can give assent to a historical fact

because of the fidelity and accuracy with which it has been trans-
mitted to us. Were this transmission faulty, "If all the long chain
of causes and effects" were composed of links different from each
other and without any relation to the original, we should never
accept the validity of historical fact. The proofs, however, of historical facts have in all cases resembled one another; and the mind
has thus accepted the facts of history without requiring that they
be repeated. For Hume, even "a long chain of argument" does not
diminish the "original vivacity" as much as it might be diminished
were the links in the argument composed of different and contrary
parts. Then the mind would have to accommodate new evidence
in judging each historical fact and would be hard pressed to decide what was fact and what was not. Yet Hume later admits that
a "long chain of objects" can diminish the evidence for an original
idea or historical fact (*Treatise*, I, iii, 13; 146, 154).

In conjunction with this metaphor of the chain, Hume often
describes the mind in terms of Newtonian and physical concepts.
The mind becomes capable of performing certain feats that are
analogous to the activity of man: "the mind runs easily along
them, jumps from one part to another with facility, and forms but
a confus'd and general notion of each link" (*Treatise*, I, iii, 13;
146). Hume also writes of the mind "passing" or "carrying" certain ideas. This movement in the mind is caused by the principle
of associationism; the metaphor would suggest that the principle
operates by means of the mind very much the same way that
Newton's laws of motion operate in the external world.

In Section I of this chapter, a master-slave metaphor called attention to the relation in Humean psychology between reason and
passion: "Reason is, and ought only to be the slave of the passions. . . ." That metaphor is a complete reversal of one Hume
used earlier in the section "Of the sceptical and other systems of
philosophy." Hume had pointed out that nature and habit soon
break the force of skeptical doubts and do not lead man to Pyrrhonistic skepticism. Likening reason to a monarch and skepticism
to its enemy, Hume says that "Reason first appears in possession
of the throne, prescribing laws, and imposing maxims, with an
absolute sway and authority. Her enemy, therefore, is oblig'd to
take shelter under her protection, and by making use of rational
arguments to prove the fallaciousness and imbecility of reason,
produces, in a manner, a patent under her hand and seal. This

patent has at first an authority, proportion'd to the present and immediate authority of reason, from which it is deriv'd."

The metaphor now changes to an expression of a contest between skeptical reasonings and dogmatic reasonings, whose authorities are equally diminished in their encounters. Neither reason nor skepticism can or should gain complete ascendancy in the human mind. Hume does not facilely suggest that man should synthesize the two, but that he must and always does yield to the "course of nature." The passions are part of the "course of nature," and Hume could easily say of skepticism, as he said of reason, that "scepticism is, and ought only to be the slave of the passions. . . ." While reason and skepticism may be enthroned at one time and enslaved at the next, they cannot and should not totally dominate the mind (see *Treatise*, I, iv, 2; 186–87, 415).

Several other metaphors, too numerous and often trivial, appear consistently throughout the *Treatise;* and a brief mention of one will perhaps indicate the manner in which Hume conceptualized certain philosophical problems. What might be loosely called a "combat" metaphor describes the struggle between the passions and reason. Hume suggests that the mind might very well be a battlefield in which battles are won according to prejudices, convictions, or impressions. This is the metaphor of the introduction, where Hume, in speaking of the disputes in philosophy, observes that eloquence, not reason, often wins the battles: "The victory is not gained by the men at arms, who manage the pike and the sword; but by the trumpeters, drummers, and musicians of the army." Of course, the approach to the study of human nature is likened to an attack upon a major power center. This metaphor implies that Hume thinks his method capable of putting down or of solving traditional philosophical problems. By winning the battle against shibboleths and metaphysical slogans, the philosopher of human nature can erect a science of human nature upon a new and secure foundation.

Considerably later, in closing his discussion of the passions, Hume varies the metaphor: "I shall observe, that there cannot be two passions more nearly resembling each other, than those of hunting and philosophy, whatever disproportion may at first sight appear betwixt them. . . . To make the parallel betwixt hunting and philosophy more compleat, we may observe that tho' in both cases the end of our action may in itself be despis'd, yet in the

heat of the action we acquire such an attention to this end, that
we are very uneasy under any disappointments, and are sorry
when we either miss our game, or fall into any error in our reasoning" (*Treatise*, II, iii, 10; 451–52).

Searching for another parallel, Hume finds that the passion of
gaming creates pleasure "from the same principles as hunting and
philosophy" (*ibid.*). The implication is clear: philosophy involves
the seeker after truth or the lover of knowledge so strongly in its
problems or objectives that he fails to realize the ultimate effect
of, for example, skepticism or dogmatism. Much of the pleasure of
philosophy lies in the manner by which one arrives at conclusions
about the nature of man or the structure of the universe. The conclusions about the nature of man or the structure of the universe
may not be pleasant when reached, but the intense pleasure of
philosophical study counteracts any attempt to anticipate undesirable consequences.

While Hume began his *Treatise* with this "combat" metaphor
and emphasizes struggles throughout, he chooses quite another
metaphor for the conclusion, that of the verb "to anatomize,"
which Dr. Johnson defined as "to lay any thing open distinctly,
and by minute parts." This metaphor was popular during the
eighteenth century, and Hume used it upon several occasions,
perhaps most notably in the *Dialogues concerning Natural Religion*. Of the function or duty of a philosopher, Hume writes:

The anatomist ought never to emulate the painter: nor in his accurate
dissections and portraitures of the smaller parts of the human body,
pretend to give his figures any graceful and engaging attitude or
expression. There is even something hideous, or at least minute in the
views of things, which he presents; and 'tis necessary the objects shou'd
be set more at a distance, and be more cover'd up from sight, to make
them engaging to the eye and imagination. An anatomist, however, is
admirably fitted to give advice to a painter; and 'tis even impracticable
to excel in the latter art, without the assistance of the former.
(*Treatise*, III, iii, 6; 620–21)

The anatomist, or philosopher, having an exact knowledge of the
workings of the human mind and its passions, can suggest ways in
which all mankind can improve itself. Man must understand the
"springs and principles" of human nature in order to create "*prac-*

tical morality," to which the abstract speculations of the philosopher must always be subservient.

Hume was the first to follow his own advice. When the abstract speculations of the *Treatise* failed to become popular in the eighteenth century, he sought to express other ideas in a medium more accessible than a philosophical treatise: the essay.

CHAPTER 3

The Moral Sciences:
Ideas in Search of a Form

I Literature: Rhetoric and Emotion

H UME addressed himself to the problem of essay writing in
the second volume (1742) of *Essays, Moral and Political.*
In a short piece entitled "Of Essay Writing" which appeared only
in that 1742 edition,[1] Hume commented upon the sparsity of intelligent conversation in the "civilized" world and observed that
"Men of Letters" were taking part in daily converse with the rest
of mankind and that the "Men of the World" were borrowing
their topics of conversation from books. To the improvement of
the alliance between the "learned and conversible Worlds," Hume
devoted his essays: "I know nothing more advantageous than such
Essays as these with which I endeavour to entertain the Public. In
this View, I cannot but consider myself as a Kind of Resident or
Ambassador from the Dominions of Learning to those of Conversation; and shall think it my constant Duty to promote a good
Correspondence betwixt these two States, which have so great a
Dependence on each other" (*Works*, IV, 368). This particular
kind of immodesty was fairly common in eighteenth-century essays; in addition, Hume thoroughly believed not only in the necessity of enlightenment but also in the expansion of the role of
the intelligent man in human affairs.

One essay in particular bears the mark of Humean skepticism
about the value of emotionalism as a means of improving the conversation among mankind. An essay "Of the Delicacy of Taste and
Passion" (1741) notes a corollary between a *"delicacy* of *passion"*
and a *"delicacy of taste."* By the term "delicacy of passion," Hume
means what we would today call "excessive sentimentality." People subject to this "delicacy of passion" permit the smallest event
to affect both their senses and their sensibilities in a manner dis-

proportionate to the stimuli which called forth the passion.[2] If I may be permitted an anachronism, Uncle Toby in Sterne's *Tristram Shandy* exemplifies what Hume called a "delicacy of passion."

A "delicacy of taste" is similar to a delicacy of passion, except that its sphere of operation is esthetics, not manners. A person given to a "delicacy of taste" would be, in modern terms, a hyperesthete, one led into raptures at the experience of any poem or painting; he is incapable of what has been called "the art of discrimination,"[3] an ability to distinguish the competent from the excellent. Of the esthete's reaction to a poem or painting, Hume remarks that "nor are the masterly strokes perceived with more exquisite relish and satisfaction, than the negligences or absurdities with disgust and uneasiness" (*Works*, III, 92). In the beginning of his essay, Hume had found a "cool and sedate" temper preferable to one afflicted with a "delicacy of passion"; but he finds "delicacy of taste" worthy of being cultivated while a "delicacy of passion" is to be avoided or remedied. To be cured of this excessive sentimentality, we should cultivate a "higher and more refined taste."

Oddly enough, what Hume is proposing is a paradox: by improving one's delicacy of taste, one eventually does not succumb to trivial and frivolous things or events. The improvement of taste eliminates, in effect, grossness and oversensibility. The mind, by cultivating its resources, learns to differentiate between the kinds of stimuli which had previously evoked a lavish response. By learning to perceive the quality of difference between two events, one is able to understand and to appreciate more fully the "polite arts." The mind becomes accustomed to a keener, more complex variety of stimuli than it had hitherto been capable of.

Apparently unsatisfied with this first attempt at a definition of taste, Hume returned to the topic in 1757 in the essay "Of the Standard of Taste" in *Four Dissertations*.[4] In common with much of his procedure, Hume emphasizes the different definitions applied to the term "taste" in different contexts, and he makes no attempt to assert or to identify an absolute standard of taste. He considers the ways in which the experience of an individual can substantially alter subsequent perceptions and judgments, but he is quick to separate perception and judgment. The method of the critic, in suggesting a standard of taste, may be adversely affected

by his subjective experience. Hume does not, however, forsake
certain predispositions: "where the ideas of morality and decency
alter from one age to another, and where vicious manners are described, without being marked with the proper characters of
blame and disapprobation; this must be allowed to disfigure the
poem, and to be a real deformity" (*Works*, III, 282). As Professor
Cohen has suggested,[5] Hume's own method invalidates that judgment; despite one's inability or incompetence to evaluate works of
art alien to one's moral and social code, the judgment is still made.

No absolute standard of taste exists in nature, but standards of
taste by which one can judge works of art are the product of experience and contemplation. The duty of the critic is, therefore, to
establish standards of taste based upon experience and historical
reliability. A standard of taste, according to Hume, will reconcile
the various sentiments men may have when regarding an alleged
work of art. Into this standard of taste he both admits and rejects
general opinion. Common sense, Hume affirms, leads men to prefer Milton to John Ogilby and Addison to Bunyan; but the same
common sense, conditioned by the empirical method of literary
inquiry, can provide in a different age contrasting yet valid conclusions about a work of art. Hume's standard of taste is not so
much a standard as a method for discovering what the standards
of one's age are, of ascertaining the intensity with which one responds to a given work, and of revealing the particular qualities of
a work that make it distinguished.

Hume's contributions to theories of taste are not easy to miss in
an age which emphasized "rules" criticism and which assumed
that standards used to judge a work in one age would be valid for
another work in another age. In opposition to this assumption,
Hume posited that the would-be critic should exhibit what he defined in that early essay as a "delicacy of taste": his response to all
the components of a work of art should be both intense and general, a sentiment in which Dr. Johnson would concur. Only by the
fullest response to the work could an accurate judgment be made.
In addition, Hume insists that the method for forming these judgments should be empirical; the more experience a man has with
beauties and deformities, the more easily he will recognize them
in artistic manifestations. Hume is opposed, therefore, to the view
that notions of taste evolve from "on high." To him, the principles
of taste are universal and almost equal in all men; only a few men,

however, are qualified to judge a work of art because only a few have taken the trouble to exercise and to develop the experience necessary to a proper evaluation of art. As a result of this insistence upon method and experience, Hume will not accept as a work of art anything that requires a standard beyond those supplied by the senses and the imagination.

Some of Hume's contributions to a theory of taste are not new; his argument that a critic must be free of prejudices has been a critical cliché longer than most of us care to imagine. He affirms that *"good sense"* will vitiate the most unproductive prejudices; he recognizes the validity of preferences (one person may prefer sublimity, another raillery); and he asserts that the representations of art which most resemble our own age and country please us most. Hume is not himself free of all the qualities he condemns since he is prejudiced in favor of literary works that extoll bravery, courage, freedom, and other virtues, and since he is opposed to those that exemplify cowardice, license, chicanery, and other vices. His system of morality obtrudes upon his esthetic judgments, although he argues that words like "virtue" imply praise, while "vice" implies blame. Paradoxically, his method allows for such excrescences in any critical theory when he admits the "right" to be unable to apply all of one's critical strictures because of a fact of psychology or physiology.

Usually bracketed with "Of the Standard of Taste" is the essay "Of Tragedy," which also first appeared in *Four Dissertations*. A shorter essay than the one on taste, it tries to explain why we are pleased at the representation of sorrow, terror, and anxiety in a tragedy. In the *Treatise*, in a section entitled "Of Compassion," Hume had explained the pleasure of tragedy by appeal to a sympathy theory, arguing that the spectator's identification with the processes in the drama created a favorable, pleasant response (*Treatise*, II, ii, 7; 369). "Of Tragedy" is a considerable alteration and revision of that sympathy theory.[6]

Hume takes into account the Abbé Dubos' representation of a sympathy theory of tragedy and considers some other explanations for the pleasure derived from it. In answer to this theory Hume posits that "This extraordinary effect proceeds from that very eloquence, with which the melancholy scene is represented" (*Works*, III, 261). In describing why the sympathy theory is insufficient, Hume relies on a number of informative verbs: "excite,"

"overpower," "convert," "join," "alter," and "convey." Such elements as the forceful expression of passions and the "beauty of
oratorial numbers" in a tragedy create, because they are applied
to an interesting subject, an intense feeling of pleasure that is not
allied to any identification one makes with the characters of a
drama. He admits that tragedy is an imitation, but he argues that
imitations are always agreeable. We do realize that the tragedy is
a fiction, and this realization "softens" the passions engaged by a
tragedy and converts them into a "new feeling"—one neither sympathetic nor realistic but, for lack of a better word, adventitious.
The emotions we the spectators feel are not exactly extrinsic to the
situation which calls them forth, but they are emotions transformed by the context in which we experience tragedy. In one
sense, Hume is saying that our idea of tragedy and the pleasure it
gives us are derived from a recombination and conversion of original impressions in our minds. The imitation of tragedy on the
stage, combined with appropriate histrionics, produces pleasure in
us because the experience is different not only in kind but in degree from that of ordinary life.

The literary criticism in these two essays is rhetorical, not philological, perhaps because rhetoric was one of Hume's early concerns. As we saw above, one of the elements involved in the transformation of passions was eloquence; in the second volume of *Essays, Moral and Political,* Hume titled one essay "Of Eloquence"
(1742). Hume observes that the modern period is superior to the
ancient in philosophy but much inferior in eloquence; that England can honor its poets and philosophers, but that it has no orators to speak of. What it calls "eloquence" is simply "good sense,
delivered in proper expression" (*Works,* III, 169). The speakers
in England are temperate and calm and dare not employ the bold
figures of speech used by Demosthenes and Cicero. But Hume is
not convinced that ancient eloquence is unsuitable to the modern
temper.

Although Hume does not define eloquence denotatively, he
does give an intensive, or connotative, definition. Dr. Johnson, in
his *Dictionary,* had defined eloquence as the "power of speaking
with fluency and elegance; oratory." Hume's definition involves
more of a value judgment than Johnson's. Eloquence appeals
chiefly to the passions and can override reason because its language is not the calm and decorous appeal of "sweet reason."

Hume disputes the assumption that the "superior good sense" of the eighteenth century makes eloquence archaic or impractical: "our orators [could be] more cautious and reserved than the ancient, in attempting to inflame the passions, or elevate the imagination of their audience: But, I see no reason, why it should make them despair absolutely of succeeding in that attempt. It should make them redouble their art, not abandon it entirely" (*Works*, III, 169).

Spoken eloquence involves the use of elaborate figures of speech, elevated rhetoric, a voice of energy and modulation. Its appeal is visceral, not intellectual; therefore, eloquence is judged both qualitatively and quantitatively. When the principles, or passions, or sentiments in man are properly stimulated, he responds with satisfaction and is able to distinguish works of genius from works of capricious wit. This judgment is even more true of eloquence than the liberal arts: the more an eloquent speaker can move the public or a great mass of people, the greater he is.

While Hume is saying that an eloquent appeal is more forceful and more pleasing than a calmly reasoned speech, he does not suggest that eloquence should be the means by which the emotions of men are falsely swayed. Even the most impassioned speech is not exempt from order and coherence, but the method of presentation ought to make the most of an effective rhetorical structure. And, of course, Hume confines eloquence to those subjects for which it is fitted; the principle of decorum is almost an accepted fact.

In this essay, Hume is interested, as he is in other essays, in differentiating among various subjective responses to an event, particularly the response of a large group of people when contrasted to a small group or an individual. What is appropriate in one circumstance is not in another, for reactions to any appraisal of events become more subtle when they are individualized. This point is reiterated close to the beginning of one of his longer essays, "Of the Rise and Progress of the Arts and Sciences" (1742), in which Hume observes that "those principles of causes, which are fitted to operate on a multitude, are always of a grosser and more stubborn nature, less subject to accidents, and less influenced by whim and private fancy, than those which operate on a few only" (*Works*, III, 175).

Hume's esthetic suggests two different degrees of events to engage our sentiments, our taste, our passions. Some events are large-scaled, perhaps even coarse; their appeal is to large multitudes, and they must be evaluated in terms of the efficaciousness of that appeal. These large-scaled esthetic events, designed for masses of people, would be inappropriate in the parlor or in a man's closet. Perhaps an event of this kind could be scaled down, as one might take the sentiments found in a piece of rhetorical eloquence and fit the sentiments into the rhetoric of a short poem. The intensity of the esthetic event and its appeal are not so much reduced as transformed into a medium more appropriate for small audiences. An esthetic event of this kind allows for, even requires, a subtilized response from an individual or a small group of people.

More important than the differentiation of esthetic responses is Hume's insistence upon the emotional value of the work of art. In fact, Hume has all but excluded truth as a value from an esthetic construct; a work of art is judged not so much on its fidelity to "truth" or "reality," or on some other hard-worked cliché, but on the quality and extent of emotional response it elicits from the spectators. The orthodox theory of "imitation" or "mimēsis," so essential to most critics of the seventeenth and eighteenth centuries, has been discredited in favor of one which emphasizes creativity, uniqueness, and suggestivity. Where possible, art was to be measured by empirical standards. The emotions pertinent to or elicited by the work of art under consideration were the guides. Admittedly, Hume hazarded some false psychological assumptions; but he insisted that a work of art was not something sifted from the "rules" but an independent emotional experience involving the spectator temporarily in emotions or passions different from those of everyday experience.

II Morals: Diversity and Humanity

The essays discussed in the previous section represent Hume's inquiry into literary theory. While we need not bother ourselves excessively about what kind of essays they are (literary, political, or moral), we can note that almost any of Hume's essays could be classified as "moral" in the eighteenth-century sense of that term. Pope's *Epistles to Several Persons* were titled *Moral Essays* and comprehended a wide variety of subjects. The third definition Dr. Johnson gave in his *Dictionary* for moral was "popular; customary; such as is known or admitted in the general business of life."

Yet, in reading Hume's "moral essays," we need not give such a wide meaning to the term. Hume's "moral essays" could include "Of the Liberty of the Press," but the contents would seem to define it more as a political essay. Hume never specified which of his essays was "moral," but it is worthwhile to note that any number of topics could be considered under that term.

One of the recurring questions of the eighteenth century—or any century for that matter—was that of man's "dignity" or "meanness"; and Hume addressed himself to this subject in an essay "Of the Dignity or Meanness of Human Nature" (1741). Originally, the essay was entitled "Of the Dignity of Human Nature," which gives us a clue to Hume's sentiments. Stating that sentiments favorable to mankind are more likely to promote virtue than misanthropy, while sentiments denigrating mankind promote meanness, Hume is persuaded that the dispute concerning the dignity or meanness of human nature is more often verbal than real. He agrees that no one would deny the actual difference between vice and virtue, wisdom and folly, or other polarized qualities. In spite of these determinable differences, we affix blame or merit not by appeal to a "fixed unalterable standard in the nature of things" but by comparison. When we compare ourselves to animals, we are naturally overwhelmed with our superiority. Yet we may exalt our notions of the excellencies of man beyond even what we experience in ourselves, a vice to which Pope called attention in the *Essay on Man*. Comparisons, however, induce contempt for man because we find only a few whom we consider wise, virtuous, or beautiful. Without appealing to an absolutist standard of excellence, Hume points out that the appellations of "wise" or "beautiful" are the products of comparison; were the very lowest sort of mankind as wise as Cicero or Bacon, we could still find few "wise" men on earth.

Hume is apparently trying to tread a dangerous ground between absolutism and relativism. His success is perhaps tenuous, but he had been preparing the reader for the only proper kind of comparison, to his way of thinking: the principles by which humans are moved to decisions or judgments. To Hume, much of the dispute in the controversy is linguistic; and he cannot understand, for example, those who maintain that self-love, in any of its forms, pervades all of man's acts. Should a misanthrope persist in the linguistic error of calling kindness to others self-love, he would have to admit that this kindness has an immense influence upon human actions. The fallacy lies, Hume maintains, in assuming that all acts of virtue or friendship must have a selfish motive.

Applying the same logic here that he did to theories of causality, Hume argues that the virtuous sentiment precedes and produces pleasure; the virtuous sentiment does not derive from the pleasure. On another level, it is argued that virtuous men are not unreceptive to praise and have therefore been pronounced vain. But who would ascribe an act of any kind entirely to one motive? Vanity and virtue, Hume alleges, are interconnected; and the love of fame stemming from one's praiseworthy actions is similar to and intermixed with the love of praiseworthy actions for their own sake. Hume concludes that the love of glory for virtuous deeds certainly indicates an actual love of virtue. The implication is clear: how could one not love virtue if he loved the acclaim one received for being virtuous?

In positing that words which describe deeds cannot go beyond the available evidence, which he was to do again in the *Enquiry concerning the Principles of Morals*,[7] Hume seems to be simplifying any discussion of ethics. He was doing that and more: he was raising questions about the nature of language and its normative function. Language could not have some elusive meanings available only to those gifted with some kind of linguistic "second sight." Words would have to mean what they seemed to mean, not someone's idea of what a word "really" meant. Interlaced with this skepticism about a hidden meaning or motive behind the words one uses to describe moral acts is an awareness of the logical danger of confusing the meaning of a word with what it suggests. Language, Hume says, should not suggest more meanings than the evidence warrants.

This position is firmly developed, by means of an excellent example, in the essay "Of National Characters" (1748). By this term Hume meant those qualities we assign to an individual because of his geographical or cultural origin. Quashing the assumption that these physical causes could have some effect upon the formation of national character, Hume asserts that even the most superficial observer would realize that a nation's character was the result of moral causes. When we attribute national character to physical causes, we do so from an inclination to invest a general term with more authority than it could reasonably command. We allow the

contiguity of certain physical phenomena to a people to impose
upon their culture certain presumptions about their moral qualities (people living in hot countries are more warm-blooded than
those living in cold countries, etc.). For Hume, language can convey precise information only when used with an awareness of its
invitation to exaggeration.

One of the ways in which Hume tries to make his analysis precise is by relying upon historical example and not upon a priori
precepts. In "Of National Characters," for example, all of the presumptions made in the name of national character are subjected
to a historical methodology. Generalizations which do not fit the
lessons of history are thus discarded. While this methodology,
rather obvious to us, works well when Hume's skepticism restrains
his personal inclinations, it is not so successful when he is bested
by his sense of national pride. The essay "Of Polygamy and Divorces" (1742) incorporates Hume's attention to linguistic impro-
prieties and to the historical methodology, but it also concludes
that "The exclusion of polygamy and divorces sufficiently recommends our present EUROPEAN practice with regard to marriage"
(*Works*, III, 239). Hume arrives at this conclusion by his reluctance to admit "barbarism" into the workings of human nature
and from his aversion to tyranny in any form.

To approach the subject of polygamy and divorces in a casual
essay as if it required subtle philosophical discriminations would
perhaps be inappropriate in the eighteenth century. But Hume
employs a generalization in this essay that lapses from his customary perspicuity: "To render polygamy more odious, I need not
recount the frightful effects of jealousy, and the constraint in
which it holds the fair-sex all over the east." Relying even on the
scanty information about the East available to him, Hume gener-
alizes beyond his evidence. The available literature from and of
the East thoroughly indicated that sexual jealousy was an emotion
peculiar to the Western, or European, world. In some of the editions of this essay, Hume even quoted a piece of Turkish wisdom,
without realizing that it implied an absence of sexual jealousy in
Eastern nations. A Turkish ambassador in France, Hume reports,
found the Turks simpletons in comparison to the Christians: "*We
are at the expense and trouble of keeping a seraglio, each in his
own house: But you can ease yourselves of this burden, and have
your seraglio in your friends' houses*" (*Works*, III, 234n.). Hume

defends European womanhood against this ungallant observation, but he is still blind to the apparent absence of jealousy, or at least the Western kind of jealousy, in Eastern nations. In this instance, his nationalistic pride overwhelms philosophic detachment.

Hume's observations about divorce are perhaps more cogent, if his premises are accepted. He makes the common objection to divorce because of its effects on children, but his second argument premises that males, in spite of their delight in liberty, will adjust to necessity, and, eventually, the proximity of their spouses will create harmony and friendship.[8] Marriage chiefly subsists, not by love, but by friendship. To this rather constrained sense of marriage, he adds the proviso that only those people whose interests are closely allied should marry. Hume's purpose in the essays was to vindicate Western preferences in regard to marriage and to justify monogamy. He succeeded only by discarding some of his skeptical inclinations and by short-changing the reader on historical examples. He used literary and historical examples as equally forceful, a mixture of evidences he seldom committed.

Hume's interest in historical problems may have provided the impetus for a set of four essays, all written in the first person, discussing the positions of certain Classical philosophies: "The Epicurean," "The Stoic," "The Platonist," and "The Sceptic" (1742). The intention of these essays, Hume noted, "is not so much to explain accurately the sentiments of the ancient sects of philosophy, as to deliver the sentiments of sects, that naturally form themselves in the world, and entertain different ideas of human life and of happiness" (*Works*, III, 197n.). In them, Hume adopts both the rhetoric and the logic of the various sects; and he often satirizes the ideas he is representing.

The image Hume presents of Epicureanism is typical of his century.[9] Man is envious of nature because it produced him and must always be the source of creative inspiration and energy; however, he cannot possibly equal its achievements. To the Epicurean, nothing is so ridiculous as philosophers' attempts to produce artificial happiness out of reason and reflection. The human mind and its bodily confinements are not self-sufficient in the pursuit of pleasure, which, when it comes to the Epicurean, all too quickly departs. Cheerful discourse, not reason, leads to wisdom; and men are often led astray from the correct pursuit of pleasure by the love of glory. Life's ephemerality should impel them to the most intense gratification possible for their senses.

Epicureanism suffers no great injustices in this summary of the ideas Hume presents as those of that sect. The rhetoric for this literary occasion, however, calls attention to what Hume must have considered absurdities in Epicurean ideology. The excesses, ironically emphasized by exclamation points, imply that Epicureanism is more of a pose than a position; that it sacrifices logic and good sense to its own image of itself.[10] Confusing esthetics with ethics, the Epicurean throws his life away in vain pursuit of pleasure, foiled by a term he never defines. Although Epicurus considered *ataraxia* ("tranquillity") the highest goal of pleasure, Hume never mentions this contemplative side of Epicurean thought; he prefers to caricature Epicureanism with the exotic flowers of an over-fertile rhetoric: "But see, propitious to my wishes, the divine, the amiable PLEASURE, the supreme love of GODS and men, advances towards me. At her approach, my heart beats with genial heat, and every sense and every faculty is dissolved in joy; while she pours around me . . . all the treasures of the autumn. . . . O! for ever let me spread my limbs on this bed of roses, and thus, thus feel the delicious moments with soft and downy steps, glide along" (*Works*, III, 199–200).

After reading this essay, we are not surprised to read in Hume's last work, the *Dialogues concerning Natural Religion*, that "the old EPICUREAN hypothesis . . . is commonly, and I believe, justly, esteemed the most absurd system, that has yet been proposed . . ." (*Dialogues*, 182). Although the speaker in this instance, Philo, representing Hume's views, alludes to the Epicurean cosmogony, Hume would no doubt include the Epicurean ethic.

Compared to the Epicurean, the Stoic fares much better in Hume's representation. The Stoic argues that man's essential difference from the brutes—his "affinity with superior beings"—urges him into art and industry; and nature supplies him with unfinished materials to refine for his own use and convenience. Man should acknowledge nature's beneficence, not be content merely to accept it, and should seek both physical and mental self-improvement. Human skills, when developed, lead to happiness, the purpose of all human industry. But the pleasures of the Stoic

are not those of the Epicurean: only those pleasures and enjoy-
ments acquired by labor and industry are permanent; all else is
transitory. The man who seeks pleasure on a bed of roses soon
discovers that his "pleasure" also creates indolence, disgust, and
anxiety. Happiness must result from security, and the achievement of wisdom requires compassion. The reward of virtue is celestial and earthly glory.

The presentation of Stoic doctrine is relatively favorable, and
the rhetoric is not fixed upon any ironic framework. Still, Stoicism
is not free of excesses, some of which are similar to those of Epicureanism. Like that philosophical sect, Stoics make too much of
the harmony of minds and of the effect that personal virtue may
have on other individuals. Devoting themselves to the pursuit of
virtue, they become more interested and more involved in the in-
tricacies, rather than in the object, of that pursuit. Hume's strongest criticism seems, however, to be devoted to the implied denigration of human nature in Stoicism. Although exalting man for
struggle and triumph, for vindicating the intelligence with which
nature equipped him, Stoicism makes man too much a slave to
nature. Thus, the consolations it offers must militate against precepts which are sometimes self-vitiating. Nor should the consolations of philosophy have a strictly utilitarian value, with all activity subordinated to the principle of self-betterment. In spite of its
high goals and higher pretensions, Stoicism, as Hume paints it,
can exert a pressure on man that turns his desire to improve himself into a necessity for glorifying himself.

Even the slightest acquaintance with Hume would not permit
any reader to think of him as a Platonist; that the Platonist, then,
should get short shrift is no surprise. This essay, barely over one
thousand words and the shortest of the four, has its speaker expressing no surprise that the vicissitudes of human nature should
be so extreme. To the Platonist, the activities of human life are
but a tiny portion of the divine; and the furious pursuit of popu-
larity and of sensual indulgence hardly equips the mind for its
most solemn function: the contemplation of the Supreme Being.
The Epicurean's pursuit of pleasure leads finally and inevitably to
a sense of guilt that is exacerbated by a worn-out body. The Stoic
is little better: he can hardly wait for the popular recognition of
his own, highly touted virtue. Because Stoics devote themselves to
the products of men's hands and men's minds, they forget the

adoration due the Divinity. The most perfect products are those of the mind, and what is a more natural course for man, in the quest for true virtue and true wisdom, than to confine himself to the contemplation of the perfect? Of all examples of virtue pretended to by man, the most worthy is the Deity.

Each of these three essays—"The Epicurean," "The Stoic," and "The Platonist"—ends with some remark about the purpose of the Deity in human affairs. The Epicurean envisions a god, "if any governing mind preside," who would be satisfied to see his creatures achieving their purpose on earth—the pursuit and attainment of pleasure. For this end, and no other, the Epicurean holds, was man created; the knowledge that our pleasure would give our creator pleasure sustains us and frees us. In opposition to this view, the Stoic, who is more certain of the being of God, finds satisfaction in virtue on earth. The man of morals, having done his best on earth, is appropriately unconcerned with the promises extended in the concept of a life beyond death. He acknowledges the benevolence of the creator and is content with the one opportunity he has to add luster to the name of virtue. These mild endorsements of a Supreme Being are quickly overshadowed by the brief homily of the Platonist, whose discourse always informs his predecessors of the omnipotence and omniscience of God. Man's chief virtue is the contemplation of the perfection of God; and in a state beyond this life, he shall enlarge the dimensions of that contemplation. Man must not be misled by his own stupidity into thinking that pleasure lies elsewhere and that his task on earth, a task he can never complete, will become the occupation of an eternity.

The increasing insistence upon the role of a Supreme Being in each of these philosophical sects, as Hume represents them, does not culminate with a rationalistic apotheosis in the last of the four essays, "The Sceptic." The first three essays make important revelations about Hume's position on certain ethical problems, and their importance is heightened by the criticism made of these other doctrines in "The Sceptic." This essay, about as long as the other three combined, is certainly livelier than they are.

The Stoic argues that philosophers pay too much attention to principles and too little to the variety of operations in nature; they are, therefore, most suspect when reasoning about the methods of attaining happiness. The Skeptic questions that human nature and its urge towards happiness can be explained by any one set of general principles. More importantly, he raises questions about the functions and duties, if any, of a philosopher. One principle which philosophy teaches is that allegedly innate properties have no bearing on the value-terms assigned to things. Esthetic or ethical implications of language lie not in the object but in "the sentiment of the mind which blames or praises." A diversity of sentiments among mankind precludes universal agreement on the constituents of beauty and worthiness; this diversity of sentiment should make us aware of nature's autonomy.

No analogies can be drawn between, for example, the "truths" of celestial mechanics and the approbation one gives a work of art. The Skeptic does not think that taste, colors, and the sensible qualities are necessarily to be found within one's body; rather, they are part of the cultural inclination of the particular human being. The Skeptic does agree, however, that the "happiest disposition of the mind is the *virtuous*," which is defined as that "which leads to action and employment, renders us sensible to the social passions, steels the heart against the assaults of fortune, reduces the affections to a just moderation, makes our own thoughts an entertainment to us, and inclines us rather to the pleasures of society and conversation, than to those of the senses" (*Works*, III, 221). Men's actions are guided by constitution and temperament, not general maxims. The Skeptic concludes that virtue is always the best choice for man, but human life is so fragmented that no one should expect uninterrupted happiness—or misery.

If we can assume that the viewpoint of the Skeptic in some measure represents Hume's, then we have another of those careful attempts on his part to tread a thin line between an "objectivist" view of ethics and of esthetics and a "subjectivist" view. He is emphatically anti-objectivist, but this opposition does not automatically consign him to the subjectivist camp. Instead, Hume pushes the esthetician and the ethicist strongly down the road to a consideration of an individual's response to an act or event.

The worth of an object is derived not from any qualities it may be presumed to contain within itself, but from the passion (roughly, desire) with which we pursue it. This passion, when pronouncing judgment, does not render its verdict simply from a consideration of the object itself but from all of the circumstances and accidents which attend it. A passion is not a unique response creating a unique standard by which an object is judged; it is, instead, a concatenation of natural proclivities and custom. Thus, the philosophy of the skeptic offers no remedy for those who are born with, or into, the kind of disposition that contemns and abominates mankind. Yet who would say that any other philosophy can rehabilitate those who are ill-disposed towards the rest of mankind? The mind can perhaps be reformed by habit, but the conviction that the virtuous life is best is likely to impress only the man already virtuous.

Of this essay, John Laird, one of the better commentators on Hume, has said that it "proceeded to be rather more sceptical than Hume generally permitted himself to be on ethical subjects." [11] In fact, Hume was more skeptical in this essay about everything than in any of his other writings. The opening words of the concluding paragraph are sometimes cited as an instance of philosophical despair: "In a word, human life is more governed by fortune than by reason; is to be regarded more as a dull pastime than as a serious occupation; and is more influenced by particular humour, than by general principles" (*Works*, III, 231). We ask two questions of life and find neither answer satisfactory. If we involve ourselves in it with passion and anxiety, we find that we give it too much concern; if we resign ourselves to indifference, we miss the pleasure of the game. We waste our lives reasoning about life only to discover that life is gone and that death treats the philosopher and the fool alike. Yet the role of the philosopher, Hume concludes, offers man one of the most diverting and amusing occupations which life offers.

The somberness of this essay is not always found in the other "moral" essays. Some exhibit a light touch and reflect the amusement that the philosopher finds in whatever diversion life offers. Hume was attempting in these essays to be both Addison and Bishop Butler, to entertain and to instruct his readers, preferably at the same time. In essays like "The Sceptic," he suggested totally different ways in which one could regard the explanations offered for the esthetic or ethical value in some object. In some, he artlessly defended practices common to the European frame of mind. And, in others, he simply demolished assumptions about history or human nature that were part of the accepted opinion of his day.

III *Politics: Whig Principles and Tory Prejudices*

Hume's political thought is something of a trial for the average reader since his ideas cannot be conveniently fitted into any prescribed political ideology. In addition, the reader has to contend with an eighteenth-century vocabulary that does not always convey a concept amenable to modern standards of classification.[12] Much of Hume's political practicality derives from his moral persuasions, and he is prone to refer to social virtues as "artificial" and as distinct from "natural" virtues—the uniquely personal ones. The *Enquiry concerning the Principles of Morals* devotes some sections to considerations of moral acts involved in the social and political spheres, and almost all of the 1741–42 essays with political titles are permeated with moral judgments.

While an essay like "The Sceptic" gives the impression of a person unwilling to make judgments about the habits and peculiarities of others, we later find that Hume has no qualms about depicting the French government of Henry III as one filled with "oppression, levity, artifice on the part of the rulers; faction, sedition, treachery, rebellion, disloyalty on the part of the subjects . . ." (*Works,* III, 98). In the same essay, "That Politics may be Reduced to a Science" (1741), Hume asserts that a republican and free government whose checks and controls had little effect, and which also "made it not the interest, *even of bad men,* to act for the public good," would be absurd (*Works,* III, 99 [my italics]). Apparently, man must worry about the public good and upgrade it before he can turn his attention to the improvement of individual morality.

To neglect the principles of decency and morality is a common failing, as Hume observes in "Of the First Principles of Government" (1741): "When men act in a faction, they are apt, without shame or remorse, to neglect all the ties of honour and morality, in order to serve their party . . ." (*Works,* III, 110). These same men, however, should they form their faction on a principle of right or morality, could be unswervingly stubborn in their devotion to justice or equity. Still, the reader cannot escape Hume's implication that justice and equity derive, not from noble motives, but from a convenient rallying-point. The state will thus have a function in the formation of public morality. Virtue and a strong sense of morality, the foremost requirements for happiness, are not formed by the hard-shelled admonitions of religion or by the most subtle and refined principles of philosophy; virtue and general morality in a state "must proceed entirely from the virtuous education of youth, the effect of wise laws and institutions" (*Works*, III, 127). Peace and security in life derive from good government instead of from an abundance of material possessions and comforts. The benefits of good government and the morality of man are interdependent.

If this insistence upon a moral basis for governments seems to suggest that Hume accepted the idea of a "social contract," which he called the "original contract," then I must point out that Hume tentatively embraced the idea in the *Treatise* and quickly abandoned it. In the *Treatise*, he asserts that "government, *upon its first establishment*, wou'd naturally be suppos'd to derive its obligation from those laws of nature, and, in particular, from that concerning the performance of promises" (*Treatise*, III, ii, 8; 541). Yet he accepts only a part of the social-contract theory by maintaining "that tho' the duty of allegiance be at first grafted on the obligation of promises, and be for some time supported by that obligation" (*ibid.*, p. 542), it later becomes independent of all contracts. A formation of government upon this basis stems from the intrusion of change, such as the acquisition of wealth or power, among a body of people, requiring that some sort of human promises be made to supplement natural law.

Hume's concept of the usefulness and value of the "original contract" had itself changed when the essay "Of the Original Contract" (1748) appeared in *Three Essays, Moral and Political,* then in the third edition of *Essays, Moral and Political*. In this edition Hume admits only a rough idea of a theory attributing the origin of government to an original contract. He affirms that one cannot deny that government was formed by an original contract if this meant that men, living in the woods or deserts, voluntarily gave up their native liberty to accept certain conventions whose obviousness precluded any necessity of placing them in a formal document. Any original contract proceeded from the native equality, or something close to it, of men; or they would not otherwise willingly have abandoned their will to the authority of an established government.[13]

In a paragraph which Hume added to the posthumous edition of these essays, he argues that even this sketchy consent was imperfect and could not have been effective in establishing a regular administration. The exercises of authority required by such primitive forms of government, in which a tribe might be ruled by a chief of some kind, were unique; they had no established or preordained rules but were guided by the exigencies of each emergency. And, of course, the more this chief exercised his authority, the more accustomed people became to submitting to it. Thus, he acquired some control over them and established the custom of submission to authority.

Hume apparently had more trouble with this political concept —the origin of a government—than with any other. He quickly disposed of the idea that government arose from the will of a Deity by pointing out the pettiness into which the concept of rule by divine right extended. The formation of government had to be accounted for somehow since it was a human and not a divine institution; Hume could never free himself from the idea that some kind of agreement or inclination among people created at least the rudiments of government.

The only essay added to the posthumous 1777 edition was titled "Of the Origin of Government" and dealt with the same problem. In it, Hume alleges that, given some kind of temporary original agreement, the origin of a government was slow and erratic, that it did not spring into being by the agreement of men. For one thing (and Hume's moral sense inserts itself into the argument here), "such is the frailty or perverseness of our nature! [sic] it is impossible to keep men, faithfully and unerringly, in the paths of justice" (*Works*, III, 114). The incurable weakness of human nature tempts man into anti-social action. Even if the original cause of government had been some kind of contract, it would never have long subsisted because one man, or many, would be tempted to break the agreement for some private advantage. To circumvent large-scale antisocial action, man must establish the concept of obedience in order to support justice.

Accounting for the origin of government, Hume discovers that it must arise from the interplay of political forces, from the consolidation of habit, and from the human inclination to order and power. In fact, men ruled by the love of power can be instrumental in shaping a government. The force of their personalities and devotion to "their" state impose a kind of order upon other men by subordinating the wills of others to that of one leader. This interplay of political forces involves authority and liberty in perpetual opposition, although neither one can prevail for long, if a government is to be established and to survive.

Indeed, neither liberty nor authority can or should gain dominance. Liberty represents the perfection of a civil society, but, paradoxically, authority is necessary for it to exist, to insure that the partitions of power are justly administered. Justice itself, among other desiderata associated with liberty, may be suspended should some alien force threaten the welfare of a government which has emerged from various political forces that shaped it into something stable and reliable.

When discussing the various ways in which liberty takes shape in the world, Hume points out (in this same essay) that a sultan, while the master of the life and fortune of any one of his subjects, could not increase their taxes, any more than the French monarch, who can impose new taxes at will, could regulate and decide the lives of his subjects. The various ways in which liberty was regarded throughout the world was a topic of perennial interest to Hume, and one of the essays of 1741 bore the title "Of the Liberty of the Press." In it, Hume remarks that nothing would more astonish the foreign visitor to England than the liberty of the press and the journalistic censure attendant upon every decision made by the crown or by Parliament. To Hume's mind, the mixed form of government, one neither totally monarchical nor entirely republican, accounts for this liberty more than any fact.[14] So long as the republican part of England's government can prevent its being overwhelmed by the monarchical, the liberty of the press will be allowed to continue, for liberty of the press is one of the strongest props of republicanism.

Hume's attitude toward what he called a "mixed form of government" was one of his most enlightened but one also misunderstood by those in his century who wanted him classified as either Tory or Whig, so that they could pelt him with ready-made refutations. Hume found the mixed government of Britain to be predominantly republican although held in check by a strong monarchical tradition.[15] Although he altered his opinion in later life, in 1741 he saw the power of the crown increasing, after a long period when popular government was ideologically and politically powerful. The wealth of the monarchy, however, militated against the continued preeminence of republicanism.

In answering the question of his essay "Whether the British Government inclines more to Absolute Monarchy, or to a Republic," Hume prefers, in abstract, a monarchy to a republic in Great Britain. If the present form of mixed government is to come to an end—and Hume hopes that it will continue, even while recognizing that all governments have some terminus—he hoped it would come in the form of absolute monarchy, "the true *Euthanasia* of the BRITISH constitution" (*Works*, III, 126). Why? The dangers of popular government are far more terrible. The kind of republic Britons might get upon the dissolution of the present form is not the "fine imaginary republic, of which a man may form a plan in his closet," and indeed which Hume outlined in "Idea of a Perfect Commonwealth" (1752), but one unlikely to have any respect for justice and liberty. Hume suggests that it is better to let a new government form itself by whatever forces shape it under an absolute monarch than to permit a totally republican form to degenerate into anarchy. For this reason, Hume is frequently lined up with the Tories, who, if truth be said, would at the very least suspect the motives of a man who denied their divine-right theory as an account of the formation of monarchical government.

Toward the end of his life, however, in 1775, Hume had come to think that republicanism was sometimes the best form of government. In a letter to his nephew, also named David Hume, he judged that modern practices had corrected all the traditional, historical abuses associated with monarchies. He confessed his preference: "[Republicanism] is only fitted for a small State: And any Attempt towards it can in our [Country], produce only Anarchy, which is the immediate Forerunner of Despotism" (*HL*, II, 306 [words in brackets are conjectures by Greig]). Another immediate forerunner of despotism is revolution since it overthrows established governments and seeks to start anew. Hume is almost always on the side of an established government, assuming it is not tyrannical; and he prefers to keep it rather than substitute one uncertainty for a greater. But Hume also admired the revolution in the American colonies, thought it justified, and confessed, also in 1775, to Baron Mure of Caldwell, that "I am an American in my Principles" (*HL*, II, 303).

What is the reader to make of these seeming inconsistencies and others like them which compose Hume's political essays? The suggestion I can offer is only speculative, but such a solution seems preferable to an accusation of inconsistency and political illiteracy against Hume. Basically, Hume was a political theorist and not a politician. Custom and the frame of his mind led him into a skeptical analysis of conventional political wisdom; instead of continuing the principles beyond the a priori precepts of certain political ideologies, Hume tried to substitute an empirical methodology in both politics and economics. The essay "Of the Populousness of Antient Nations" is an excellent example of an attempt to fuse historical inquiry, skeptical doubts, and empirical conclusions.

As a philosopher, Hume found himself more at home with the theoretical constructs of political science than with the popular sentiments that over-simplified the complications of a continually emerging government. The "Idea of a Perfect Commonwealth" leaves no doubt that Hume was basically libertarian and that his personal preference was for a government that insured a high degree of individual liberty. Yet personal preferences, regardless of their propinquity, were expendable if the exigencies of government demanded it. Hume's function was to raise doubts, to propose alternatives, and to say the unpopular when necessary. To others belong the tasks of mollifying the populace and administering the nation's polity.

IV Economics: Historical Perspective and the Passions

The extent and the effectiveness of Hume's economic thought are not necessarily indicated by the quantity of his writings on economics. He wrote only nine essays that, strictly speaking, could be called economic essays: "Of Commerce," "Of Luxury," "Of Money," "Of Interest," "Of the Balance of Trade," "Of the Balance of Power," "Of Taxes," "Of Public Credit," and "Of the Jealousy of Trade." All were published in 1752 in his *Political Discourses*, except the last-named, which was published in 1758. Hume's discussion of economics is neither systematic nor thorough; nevertheless, his ideas on economics have been thought to be among the most valuable written in the eighteenth—or any—century.[16]

Since Hume was a contemporary of and adviser to Adam Smith, almost any discussion of Hume's economic thought is immediately compared to Smith's. Basically, Hume and Smith are in sympathy so far as the methodology of economic inquiry is concerned, although Smith's inquiries are much more developed. Smith is less concerned than Hume with the psychology of human beings involved in economic transactions, and Smith often assumes the "universal psychology" attributed to every man, regardless, as the saying goes, of race, creed, or color. In contrast, Hume considers variations in men's behavior; and his economic ideas belong most properly in the pattern of his other thoughts.

Hume is a transitional figure in the movement from mercantilist economic theory to classical economic theory, and he cannot be said to belong to either school. He was one of the first writers to demonstrate the interrelations of economic theory and economic practice and their further relation with social and political events. Briefly, for Hume, economics is the science of explaining the way in which money, trade, taxes, public credit, and commerce are produced by the changes in human wants, which are, in turn, affected by environment.[17]

"Of Commerce," generally regarded as Hume's most important economic essay, contains the outlines of his economic psychology, or the relationship between the state and the individual. He asserts what is commonly allowed, that "The greatness of a state, and the happiness of its subjects, how independent soever they may be supposed in some respects, are commonly allowed to be inseparable with regard to commerce; and as private men receive greater security, in the possession of their trade and riches, from the power of the public, so the public becomes powerful in proportion to the opulence and extensive commerce of private men" (*Works*, III, 288–89).

Hume admits that some exceptions may be admitted to this rule because of the variations in behavior patterns. Historically speaking, Hume continues, the state is greatest when its "superfluities" are used to increase public welfare; but, I hasten to add, Hume does not have in mind a "welfare state." Instead, he is following the psychological ideas suggested in his other works, that economic matters develop less from arbitrary laws of cause and effect, but from attitudes, customs, experiences, and habits. In keeping with his view in the *Treatise* that the passions are more often the "springs" of behavior than reason, Hume makes the passions the starting point of his economic theory. This procedure removed economics from the politics of mercantilism and centered it in the "science of human nature."

For Hume, labor is the ultimate source of wealth, and passions are the ultimate source of labor. Therefore, the passions are the ultimate source for the wealth and productions of the world. Passions, however, do not necessarily govern the way in which wealth is used. For example, poverty can occur when the means for attaining economic advantages are so simple and expedient that men are led into indolence, as they are in the Mediterranean countries. When economic advantages are not easily attained, men must have some potential profit before embarking on the dangers concomitant with production: "Men must have profits proportionable to their expense and hazard" (*Works*, III, 298). Throughout his essays, of course, Hume puts the psychology of economics in historical perspective; transactions involving capital or labor are obviously affected by the culture in which they occur.

Commerce, which arises from the pleasure of profits and the luxury they can bring, is not estimable exclusively in monetary terms: "Money is not, properly speaking, one of the subjects of commerce . . ." (*Works*, III, 309). While Hume's monetary theory is in places ambiguous,[18] it is, as the preceding sentence would suggest, dominantly classical. That is, Hume argues that the supply of money is unimportant since the prices of goods will always be proportionable to the actual quantity of money. Money, like a priori ideas, has no intrinsic value. The public may receive advantage from a greater supply of money, but it does so only during wars and in trade with other countries. Money by itself does not increase trade; and those countries accumulating the greatest wealth usually have the greatest expense.

Thus, their accumulation of money or wealth gives them no special advantage in commerce because the greater expenses producing that wealth make it possible for other countries to undersell them. Nor is the domestic happiness of the state increased by the quantity of its money. If the policy of the state works to increase the quantity of money, the result is desirable: it "keeps alive a spirit of industry in the nation, and encreases the stock of labour, in which consists all real power and riches" (*Works*, III, 315). As he had done in his earlier writings, Hume insists on the subtle distinctions necessary in economics between causes and effects: money is not a cause of plenty and happiness, but it can be an effect of labor and industry.

"Of Public Credit" is likely to be of more interest to the casual reader than most of Hume's other economic essays because Hume is specifically interested in the problems arising from and associ-

ated with the public, or national, debt. Hume's ironic opposition
to the accumulation of public debt to be paid off by other genera-
tions would give aid and comfort to modern conservatives opposed to "deficit financing": "it seems pretty apparent, that the
ancient maxims [saving great sums against any public exigency]
are, in this respect, more prudent than the modern; even though
the latter had been confined within some reasonable bounds, and
had ever, in any instance, been attended with such frugality, in
time of peace, as to discharge the debts incurred by an expensive
war" (*Works*, III, 361).

Hume, like many of his latter-day counterparts, thinks that min-
isters of state and politicians are unlikely to exercise restraint in
borrowing, a position pretty well borne out by historical evidence.
Incorporating sociological analysis and historical perspective, he
suggests that the increase of the public debt will, as a matter of
course, lead to bankruptcy and to political deterioration. Hume
ascribes the inclination towards a mounting public debt to the
"natural progress of things"; from a knowledge of the natures of
men and politicians, Hume suggests two possible consequences of
an increasing debt. One would result in what he calls the *natural
death* of public credit, as a result of governmental over-
extension; another consequence would be the *violent death* of
public credit as a result of an inability or reluctance to accept
voluntary bankruptcy and the subsequent submission of the state
to a conqueror.

The relations of a state to its neighbors form the subject of two
essays containing some of Hume's most original thought. "Of the
Balance of Trade" is an exposition of the inadequacy of mercantilist attempts to increase the internal quantity of money or commodities by imposing artificial limits on international trade.[19]
Hume argues that the amount of currency or cash in a country
tends towards an equilibrium as a result of a balance between its
exports and imports. Free trade prevents the escalation of prices
out of proportion to the prices asked in other countries. In a series
of rhetorical questions, Hume doubts the ability of a country to
maintain a disproportion between its supply of money and its
labor and commodities. He specifically questions the ability of a
state to lose its labor and industry and yet retain its gold and
silver; it need never fear losing its currency so long as its industry
and labor are maintained.

Six years later, in "Of the Jealousy of Trade," Hume was to reject the protectionist theory of international trade agreements, although he had conceded the necessity of tariffs in the earlier essay. No nation was likely to have its domestic industry damaged by the prosperity of neighbors, but Hume said he wished to go farther and to observe "that where an open communication is preserved among nations, it is impossible but the domestic industry of every one must receive an encrease from the improvements of the others" (*Works*, III, 345). Although the reader finds some evidence for Hume's doubts about the effectiveness of this principle, he can never doubt the moral outlook of Hume's economics, which found unlikely the proposition that a nation's wealth, commodities, and industry would be increased by its conquest of neighboring states.

Hume's economic views are neither easy to summarize nor to relate to modern problems. Perhaps his most important contribution to economic thought was the insistence that man ought to reason as subtly and as abstrusely on economics as he did on other branches of "moral science." That was the contention of the opening paragraphs in "Of Commerce," and Hume followed his own suggestion conscientiously. He never ignored the role of custom and habit in shaping economic changes; in fact, custom and habit were the source of all economic change. History and psychology were the means by which he attempted economic analyses, and he focused attention upon both the myths of economics, as well as upon the general principles to be derived from study of domestic and international transactions. His inquiry into economics relied upon the same tools he used to inquire into human understanding and into the principles of morals.

CHAPTER 4

Courage and Perseverance:
The Two Enquiries

I Human Understanding: The New and The Old

IN Chapter 1, we noticed the famous advertisement which Hume prefaced to the last edition of his works repudiating the philosophy of the *Treatise* and desiring the reader to regard only his later productions as representative of his thought. Today, of course, few people pay any attention to Hume's request and regard the *Treatise* as his major philosophical work, although nineteenth-century commentators tended to take Hume at his word and ignored the *Treatise*, with some notable exceptions. The editor of the standard Oxford editions of the two *Enquiries* and of the *Treatise*, L. A. Selby-Bigge, is in many ways responsible for focusing attention on both works.[1] The standard edition of Hume's philosophical works, by T. H. Green and T. H. Grose, devotes two volumes to the *Treatise* and two volumes to the bulk of Hume's other works (excluding the *History of England*). Almost one-third of the two volumes of this edition of the *Treatise* is devoted to the elaborate commentary by Professor Green, and we could hardly assert that the *Treatise* has been neglected at Hume's request.

Most commentators, however, have persisted in accepting the *Enquiry concerning Human Understanding* as a revision of the *Treatise*, an activity which Selby-Bigge's comparative tables have encouraged. And no one will deny that corollaries between the two exist, nor would anyone assert that a consideration of Hume's first *Enquiry* distinct from the *Treatise* amounts to a new discovery. Yet it is important to regard the work not so much as a recasting of the ideas of the *Treatise*, complete with appendices and reformulations, but as an independent contribution to the history of thought. Hume intended it to be considered that way, intended the same to be true of the second *Enquiry,* and the least that we can do is respect Hume's wishes until we have good reason to do otherwise.[2]

In the opening section of the first *Enquiry,* Hume proposes that the science of human nature may be approached in two ways. The first way is to regard man as a creature of action, not contemplation; philosophers who consider man as this active creature responding to active stimuli try, therefore, to represent the concept of virtue with all the eloquence and persuasiveness they can command. The second approach regards man as a reasonable rather than an active creature. The philosopher utilizing this approach wishes to set the limits by which man's nature can be scrutinized and regulated. Seeking to excite his curiosity about the fundamental principles of nature, he avoids the pose of certainty and avoids imposing standards of manners upon men. Of these two forms, the first is more likely to be popular with mankind in general because it makes few demands upon interaction with the problems and paradoxes of human life. And indeed, this "easy philosophy" enjoys a greater fame than "abstract philosophy." In spite of the facile dichotomy and the many thinkers who repair to it, nature has enjoined man to a mixed life, one of contemplation and action; to go too far to one extreme is to invite dissolution or melancholia: "Be a philosopher; but, amidst all your philosophy, be still a man" (*Works,* IV, 6; *ECHU,* 13).[3]

Hume is raising not only a legitimate question for his inquiry, but a necessary question: the way in which the discipline of philosophy and metaphysics can instill accuracy in the ordinary business of human life. Metaphysics encourages objections and disdain from the generality of mankind, as indeed bad metaphysics should. But the function of the philosopher is not to encourage the isolation of his discipline but, like Addison's *Spectator,* to bring "Philosophy out of Closets and Libraries, Schools and Colleges, to dwell in Clubs and Assemblies, at Tea-Tables and in Coffee-Houses" (#10, March 12, 1711). The mind must learn to reject certain philosophies as inherently misleading and to cultivate a skepticism proper to the vicissitudes of daily life, while avoiding that skepticism that totally subverts reflection or action. A proper skepticism is not fooled by the rhetoric of certainty any more than it is debilitated by the specter of total chaos. In opposition to the penchant of traditional philosophers, or even modern philoso-

phers, who hope, like Newton, to find some general principles of
human nature by which all actions can be predicted or explained,
Hume suggests that such an undertaking does not lie within the
province of human understanding. Events in the mind are more
linked to one another than to some general emanation from nature. The philosopher can apply his energies most properly to the
elucidation of whatever phenomena best contribute to the human
understanding of human nature.

Section II, "Of the Origin of Ideas," restates with some altera-
tions the propositions of the opening pages of the *Treatise*, and
we need not repeat the distinctions Hume makes except where the
Treatise is amplified, slighted, or corrected. He had, for example,
insisted in the *Treatise* on the term "image" to define ideas, and
the same word is implied in the first *Enquiry*. As Professor Flew
has pointed out, this inclination to think of ideas as images over-
simplifies the idea-forming activity of the mind. To justify his division between impressions and ideas, Hume posits experience as
arbiter: if we trace an idea back to its origins, we always find
that it derives from some initial, livelier impression. If a man is
deprived from birth of one of his senses, such as the sense of sight,
he can have no idea of what color means.[4]

But the main purpose of this short chapter comes, I think, in the
last paragraph, where Hume uses this admittedly faulty distinction as ammunition for an attack upon the splenetic metaphysics
of what the eighteenth century called "schoolmen." If we are confronted with a philosophical term which seems to have no meaning, a far too frequent occurrence for Hume, we should simply
inquire from what impression the idea arose. Although Hume
does not exhibit openly Locke's interest in the proper use of words
(Book III of Locke's *Essay* is entitled "Of Words"), his intentions
are similar: to fix the function of language within certain defin-
able rhetorical and logical limits.

Perhaps the most noticeable difference between the *Enquiry
concerning Human Understanding* and the *Treatise* lies in the diminished form of the observations made about the association of
ideas. Section III, "Of the Association of Ideas," consisted of three
paragraphs in the 1777 edition of the *Essays and Treatises*, although it was about six times as long in editions Hume published
during his lifetime. Hume notes that no philosopher has attempted to define the various classes of association, and he sug-

gests three: resemblance, contiguity in time or place, and cause or effect. Instead of expanding upon these possible classifications, Hume prefers to speculate about the effects the connection of ideas would have on our passions or our imaginations. That speculation constitutes the omitted portion of the 1777 edition. What reason he may have had for omitting this speculation from his final, authoritative edition can only be conjectured. In writing the *Abstract,* he thought the way in which the "author" of the *Treatise of Human Nature* made his most impressive contribution was in his use of the principle of the association of ideas. In the first *Enquiry,* this suggestion had been considerably modified; and Hume finally decided that the simple fact of the existence of the principle was as much as he cared to mention.

The application of the principle of the association of ideas to works of art is interesting. Hume asserts that the association of ideas here cannot be the loose or casual ones of ordinary experience but must command some kind of unity. The most unusual connecting principle is that of cause and effect, particularly when a historian tries to draw conclusions about the behavior of peoples and societies. Comparing the writing of history to the writing of poetry illuminates our understanding of the way in which cause and effect, as organizing principles of the poet, can call forth strong emotions in us. The mind, presented with a reorganized unity, is powerfully affected by the actual imputation the poem makes of cause and effect. The responses created by these perceptions and reflections increase our enjoyment of the work of art by heightening our sensitiveness to the rhetorical exigencies of art confronted with life. Hume leaves the fruitful topic reluctantly, and the reader of the first *Enquiry* certainly wishes for some additional exploration of this promising approach to literary criticism.

The first three sections, however insidiously provocative they may be, are nothing but a prologue for the heart of the book, Sections IV through VII.[5] In these four sections we find Hume's skepticism asserting itself both rhetorically and formally. Experience, which is the postulate for Hume's methodology, leads the inquirer into two modes of understanding which Hume represents as *"Relations of Ideas"* and *"Matters of Fact."* The first group consists of propositions which are intuitively or analytically certain; they are rhetorically tautological. The second group consists of propositions which are not certain, only possible; they are formally verifiable. Into this second class of propositions enter the skeptical doubts about the operations of the understanding. Any proposition, Hume affirms, the contrary of which is intelligible or subject to verification can never achieve certainty, only a high degree of expectancy.

This division of propositions is one of Hume's more important contributions to philosophy as well as to the development of theories of literature based upon subjective reevaluation of experiences. This dichotomy, called *Hume's Fork*,[6] is a step or two, perhaps several, away from the unsatisfactory psychology of the first three sections and of the psychological explanations of the understanding found in the *Treatise*. What Hume calls *Relations of Ideas* are propositions whose truth-value can be ascertained a priori; their validity cannot be denied without involving self-contradiction. For example, one could not assert that $2 + 2 = 5$ without contradicting the a priori axioms of arithmetic. Hume's statement about the first class of propositions is itself an a priori assertion; no experience can prove to us beyond all possibility of uncertainty that relations of ideas are self-verifying. We accept these propositions as intuitively true or as analytically certain because they are not matters of fact but of logic and rhetorical convention. To define "network" as Dr. Johnson did—"Any thing reticulated or decussated, at equal distances, with interstices between the intersections"—is to assert a tautology. In some instances the tautology can be illuminating if it contains words whose implications we comprehend.

While the problems involved in analytic propositions (what Hume calls *Relations of Ideas*) are considerably beyond the scope of this discussion, Hume's major interest was not in analytic but in synthetic propositions, ones which make an empirical assertion. The truth-value of synthetic propositions can be ascertained only a posteriori; that is, synthetic propositions must be subjected to a kind of verification they do not inherently contain. To add to the complexity of Hume's Fork, modern philosophers have pointed out that Hume's assertions about his second class of propositions are themselves a priori propositions. When Hume states "The contrary of every matter of fact is still possible; because it can never imply a contradiction, and is conceived by the mind with the same facility and distinctness, as if ever so conformable to reality," he argues a priori. That proposition itself cannot be verified by an appeal to the class of propositions it defines. From this position, Hume goes on to argue that man experiences the events of everyday life not as a manifold unity but as distinct entities. This contention is the source of one of the easy objections made to Hume's philosophy; namely, that it is atomistic and must inevitably involve itself in one of Zeno's paradoxes.

Hume has prepared the reader, however, for one of his important insights, the proper and improper use of the evidence of experience in determining matters of fact. He asks, *"What is the foundation of all conclusions from experience?"* (*Works*, IV, 28; *ECHU*, 42). The immediate answer is that our experience of causes and effects and our conclusions drawn from experience do not emanate from reason or from any activity of the understanding. When we experience a certain contiguity of events, we assume, extra-logically, that at any given time those events will exhibit a similar "causal" relationship. We experience the rising of the sun every day, and from the series of experiences we have of the rising of the sun, we act on the assumption that the sun will rise in the following days. Custom instills in us certain expectations about the natural process of events, and those expectations are usually justified.

These expectations are not logically justifiable. Regardless of the extensiveness of our experience, we cannot project an infinite series of cause and effect; we can appeal to no authority except custom to "prove" that the sun will rise tomorrow. We have experience of event X in a thousand circumstances; we "know" that X will always occur in those circumstances. This inference is the product of experience, but it defies all the processes of syllogistic logic. Any conceivable and hitherto unexperienced event can inject itself into familiar circumstances and cast to the four winds all of our assurance and certainty. Thus, we can never assert the logical irreversibility of any two connected events. Certainty is unobtainable in postulating that event X, which has occurred precisely at noon every day since recorded history, will occur tomorrow or the day after. Any number of imponderables can reverse that expectation.

The appeal to custom is the argument of Section V, "Sceptical Solution of these Doubts." Our experience, Hume states, would never be any use to us, as it plainly is, did we not function according to custom and expectancy, avoiding the harsher dictates of logic and reason. The constant conjunction of two events imposes its own autonomy upon our psyche, and we convert matters of fact, of past experience, into some workable calculus of probability. In daily life, Hume himself hardly doubted that his customary expectations would not be vindicated in the separate experiences of forthcoming days. Like other ordinary human beings, he formed certain patterns of belief, fashioned from the expectations of experience. Sufficient to contain the process of routine events, the evidence of experience was a reliable guide in discussing past matters of fact. But experience, Hume thinks, should also teach us that the unexpected is never far from our daily lives and that custom can actually prevent us from inquiring into matters taken for granted. The evidence of past experience is projected, on faith, into the future, but it should never be trusted to comprehend the unexpected, the unexpectable: man is a creature of limited and finite experience.

Before Hume turns to his discussion of the idea of necessary connection, he devotes the three short pages of Section VI to "Of Probability." The discussion of probability constituted three sections in the *Treatise*, and the new presentation is mute recognition of the difficulty of mixing psychology with philosophy. Chance, to Hume's mind, does not exist in the world since every future event has some probability. We cannot reconstruct the various causes of various events, but we do form certain beliefs about natural processes. Some causes always produce similar effects, at least upon human beings: fire always burns and water always suffocates any human being. But the relative certainty that may arise from this similarity of causes and effects may not appear in other examples. When two similar causes produce different results, we are forced to make some mental readjustments in future prognostications. Again Hume emphasizes the subjective quality of these experiences and implicitly suggests that man has little effect upon the force of events. Yet he explicitly challenges others to account sufficiently for the impact of mental uncertainty upon any system of philosophy, if they attempt to deny the validity of his assertions. Received theories of man, or of human experience, are all defective in treating such difficult subjects. Hume was unwilling to relinquish totally his insight, whatever its defects, about the subjectivity of any theories of probability.

In discussing the idea of necessary connection (Section VII),

Hume elaborates upon an argument made in the first part of Section IV; and, in the last section of the *Enquiry,* he summarizes this argument: "If we reason *a priori,* any thing may appear able to produce any thing. . . . It is only experience, which teaches us the nature and bounds of cause and effect, and enables us to infer the existence of one object from that of another" (*Works,* IV, 134–35; *ECHU,* 157).[7] Hume is concerned with both the logical and the psychological problems involved in reasoning from a set of propositions to a conclusion; and he sees the inexactitude of language as the chief obstacle to any inquiry about the limits of knowing. Nothing in "moral" communication enjoys the precision that one finds in mathematics, mainly because mathematics represents one kind of knowing and morality another kind.

The first part of this section considers the influence, if any, that volition has on the various components or organs of the body; but the immediate cause of that effect is not so easily known. Few principles in nature are more mysterious than this alleged influence of some "spiritual substance" on the "material substance" of our bodies. Applying the epistemology of public impressions and private ideas to this anomaly, Hume questions our ability to know precisely the activity of the will upon the body. This conjecture leads him to his second argument about the degrees of authority our will has over the various organs of our body.

Why, for example, should the fingers be immediately responsive to the will, but not the liver or heart? The extensiveness or power of our will can be known from experience only; no a priori assumption explains the workings of all the organs of the body. Yet even the effect of our will upon such obviously responsive organs as the fingers is not so simple as it seems. For the volition does not act immediately upon the organ concerned, but upon muscles and nerves. A series of unknown events finally produces the intended result, and we do not know the means by which it was achieved. These difficulties with the idea of volition, Hume discovers, by no means lead us to an awareness of a power within ourselves to comprehend what we call acts of the will. Hume raises the same objections against the assertion that ideas in the mind are subject to the same power or influence of the will, and also against the idea of attributing to the Deity the effects stemming from an act of the will.

Having argued that a priori knowledge of one event's causing, or not causing, another event is impossible, Hume now trains his attention on the instances of "necessary connection." His approach, in summary, is that events seem to occur uniquely, that one event follows another, but that we can never observe or experience any link between them: "They seem *conjoined,* but never *connected*" (*Works,* IV, 61; *ECHU,* 79). It would seem, then, that, since we have no experience of this "necessary connection," we are impelled to the conclusion that we can have no idea of necessary connection and that such words are without philosophical or commonplace meaning.

But such is not Hume's position, for he thinks that one approach will avoid this seemingly inescapable conclusion. The idea of "necessary connection" arises from the continued similarity and constant conjunction of certain events. This constant repetition enforces on us an expectation of recurrence and a belief that X, having always produced Y, will again do so: "This connexion, therefore, which we *feel* in the mind, this customary transition of the imagination from one object to its usual attendant, is the sentiment or impression, from which we form the idea of power or necessary connexion" (*Works,* IV, 62; *ECHU,* 80). Nothing in the original events themselves can contain the concept of "necessary connection." It must arise from the subjective reconsideration of the human mind, acting within ascertainable limits, of events whose connection is suggested but not necessitated by contiguity.

In discussing the idea of "necessary connection," Hume has again, I think, tried to walk along that thin line between "objectivity" and "subjectivity," to accept for a minute the vague implications of those words. In fact, he has tried to avoid making such a distinction since bifurcation of one's experience is both simple and simple-minded. Explicitly, he has now questioned the utility of such concepts; implicitly, he has demonstrated the confusion in which they involve even the most careful thinker. The activity of the mind in perceiving phenomenal events is itself not an isolatable event. Too, who can imagine a mind not perceiving events with which it was existentially confronted? The mind cannot refuse to perceive these events; at the least, it must receive them. Hume attempted to construct a methodology that would consider the mind both as process and participant in phenomenal events. In the act of perceiving, the mind is aware of the fact that it is perceiving and is inextricably involved with the events it observes.

The process of events in the "external world" and of events in the "mind" are, Hume implies, incapable of being totally separated; and one must take into account this condition when reasoning about human nature.

The two sections following Hume's analysis of the idea of necessary connection are entitled "Of Liberty and Necessity" (Section VIII) and "Of the Reason of Animals" (Section IX). Controversy over the freedom of the will has long been a perennial staple of philosophy, and an examination of the problem of reason in animals usually emphasizes the limitations of any analogy drawn between animals and men.[8] Hume's argument in Section VIII, that disputes over liberty and necessity are more verbal than real, is cogent; but the real interest of the section lies in his tacit preparation for the dissection of miracles. Hume regards any attempt to refute a given hypothesis on the ground that it endangers religion and morality as not only blameable but stupid. When a man inquires into the role that the Deity may play in human moral decisions, he is inviting confusion. Of the difficulties attached to this or to any inquiry about liberty and necessity, Hume ironically asserts,

These are mysteries, which mere natural and unassisted reason is very unfit to handle; and whatever system she embraces, she must find herself involved in inextricable difficulties, and even contradictions, at every step which she takes with regard to such subjects. To reconcile the indifference and contingency of human actions with prescience; or to defend absolute decrees, and yet free the Deity from being the author of sin, has been found hitherto to exceed all the power of philosophy. Happy, if she be thence sensible of her temerity, when she pries into these sublime mysteries; and leaving a scene so full of obscurities and perplexities, return, with suitable modesty, to her true and proper province, the examination of common life; where she will find difficulties enow to employ her enquiries, without launching into so boundless an ocean of doubt, uncertainty, and contradiction! (*Works*, IV, 84: *ECHU*, 103–04)

Hume's analysis of miracles exemplifies the above contention. As the reader will recall from Chapter 1, "Of Miracles" is unequivocally the most controversial thing Hume ever wrote. In addition, it contains some of his most subtle reasoning and, to the devout, some of the most frightening logic ever assembled in one short essay. A miracle Hume defines as a "violation of the law of nature" and asserts that the testimony offered in support of miracles is never totally reliable. The general assumptions of the first part of this section involve a priori maxims which nonetheless lead to ineluctable a posteriori conclusions. No testimony offered in the defense of a miracle can be sufficient to validate it, unless that testimony is itself so powerful that its falsity would be more miraculous than that very miracle which it supports.

Hume then subjects the evidence offered in support of miracles to the weight of customary experience and to the frequent variation and unreliability of the sources cited in support of the miracle. Pointing out that reports which favor the passions or religious inclinations of the reporter cannot, by definition, be impartial, Hume questions if we can actually obtain reliable evidence for miracles. Most evidence will be distorted because it is partisan; and scrupulous, impartial inquiry is unlikely. In a classic paragraph, he observes, "Upon the whole, then, it appears, that no testimony for any kind of miracle has ever amounted to a probability, much less to a proof; and that, even supposing it amounted to a proof, it would be opposed by another proof; derived from the very nature of the fact, which it would endeavour to establish."

Experience alone can invest human testimony with authority, the same experience which has regularized nature. How can we react when the experience of the laws of nature is violated by what is alleged to be a miracle? We must decide which is more extraordinary: the miracle or the testimony offered in support of it. The result is invariably inconclusive: "and therefore we may establish it as a maxim, that no human testimony can have such force as to prove a miracle, and make it a just foundation for any such system of religion" (*Works*, IV, 105; *ECHU*, 126).

Both Hume's language and his methodology are uncompromising. He has denied the validity of the usual evidence advanced in support of a miracle since that evidence satisfies none of the criteria he established for miracles. Knowing full well the eccentricities of human beings, he has suggested that human credulousness created more miracles than any other single cause. The evidence that Hume finds acceptable in supporting miracles is more quantitative than qualitative. Near the end of the essay, he allows that a sufficient uniformity of agreement about a violation of the laws of nature would validate a claim to miraculousness. But the kind of events men offer as miracles are so narrow and chaotic that empirical credibility cannot be extended them. The most persuasive argument that Hume uses, however, is one Bertrand Russell was to use two hundred years later:[9] that miracles invoked in support of one system of religion almost always conflict with or contradict the miracles of another—and conflicting assertions cannot both be true. So many witnesses oppose the various miracles of opposing sects that the testimony destroys itself. How is one to decide among the evidence offered for a countless number of miracles? In the land of the blind, the one-eyed man is king; but we are all blind in weighing the evidence for miracles.

Hume's concluding remarks are appropriately ironic. Approvingly, he quotes Bacon on the suspiciousness of "relations" which depend upon religion, observing that Bacon's reasoning "may serve to confound those dangerous friends or disguised enemies to the *Christian Religion,* who have undertaken to defend it by the principles of human reason" (*Works,* IV, 107; *ECHU,* 126–27). Religion, Hume asserts, is founded on faith; its only defense, if it need one, is faith. Considering the Pentateuch, he finds that we are presented with a book written in a barbarous age by ignorant people. It records events long past even testimonial verification and is full of any number of miracles, prodigies, and incomprehensibles. "I desire any one," Hume says, "to lay his hand upon his heart, and after a serious consideration declare, whether he thinks that the falsehood of such a book, supported by such a testimony, would be more extraordinary and miraculous than all the miracles it relates . . ." (*Works,* IV, 108; *ECHU,* 128). Our own experience will not permit us to assert a series of empirical propositions we have, in fact, never experienced. The acceptance of the contrary more easily coincides with our natural inclination and experience than the miraculous events recorded in the Pentateuch, or any other work for that matter.

Remembering one of Hume's prior observations (page 92) that began "Upon the whole," the eighteenth-century reader, as well as the modern reader, might have found one of the last sentences a real shocker: "So that, upon the whole, we may conclude, that the *Christian Religion* not only was at first attended with miracles, but even at this day cannot be believed by any reasonable person without one" (*Works,* IV, 108; *ECHU,* 128). If the testimony for a miracle has never amounted to a probability, still less to a proof, and if no one can believe the Christian religion without accepting the validity of at least one miracle, the conclusion of the syllogism is inescapable: the Christian must believe what can never be proved and must assent to a "continued miracle in his own person." He must believe the contrary of what experience and even common sense tell him. Small wonder that Hume was regarded, and still is in some quarters, as a dangerous infidel, although much of the preceding argument would probably not shock those who followed the Calvinistic evaluation of reason. Small wonder, too, that some modern commentators fail to take Hume seriously.[10] Yet Hume's position, when thought through, actually strengthens the validity of the self involved in the personal experience of religion. Religion must be strong in a man's mind and heart, not by laws, customs, platitudes, or logic, but by a conscious faith. Religion without faith is a fraud; and faith, according to Hume, without miracles is impossible.

Throughout this section of the first *Enquiry,* the reader sees Hume's skepticism at work on a topic too often clouded by sentimentality or taboos. He treats miracles as what they have pretended to be—a particular branch of knowledge; and acceptance of them is wisdom of the most exalted kind. But they cannot be dealt with by any of the rules which conventionally govern inquiries into human phenomena. If miracles are amenable to the logic and reason which guide inquiries into history, for example, then they are incapable of probability or proof. Miracles and other events that involve faith do not belong to ordinary methods of discourse but must achieve whatever validity they have by the rules of faith. They have not the force of knowledge and should not be accepted as knowledge.

Any sections following "Of Miracles" would almost have to be anticlimatic. They very well may be, but they shouldn't. Section XI, "Of a Particular Providence and of a Future State," is mistitled since providence and futurity are hardly mentioned. The original title, which appeared in only the first edition, was "Of the Practical Consequences of Natural Reason," a designation which clarifies its relation to "Of Miracles." In it, Hume poses as the recipient of the skeptical observations of a friend, whose principles, however curious and relevant, he cannot accept. This pose is strategic since Hume would have been ill advised to spend one section demolishing empirical arguments for miracles, only to follow it with a demonstration of the difficulties inherent in the analogical method of reasoning upon natural religion. This is what the "friend" does; and Hume, instead of disagreeing, supplements the arguments against natural religion that his friend makes. The chief mistake in analogical reasoning lies in the human penchant to attribute to the Deity the same conduct and intelligence we have. The result is unbounded conjecture, and inquiry from effect to cause based upon this analogy. Since the argument here is one expanded by Philo in the *Dialogues concerning Natural Religion,* we need not examine it thoroughly.

Hume does, however, take this opportunity to vindicate the practical harmlessness of philosophical inquiry: "I think, that the state ought to tolerate every principle of philosophy; nor is there an instance, that any government has suffered in its political interests by such indulgence. There is no enthusiasm among philosophers; their doctrines are not very alluring to the people . . ." (*Works,* IV, 121; *ECHU,* 143). The only exception Hume makes for this generalization is the prevalence of doctrines or reasonings manifestly inimical to the best interests of scientific inquiry or of political uniformity.[11]

Hume's strategy is similar in Section XII, the last, "Of the Academical or Sceptical Philosophy," where he alleges (perhaps truthfully) that "The *Sceptic* is another enemy of religion." The essay contains, however, Hume's best statement of the proper role of the skeptic. Cartesian skepticism withers quickly before Hume's blast at the a priori assumptions it involves, while the skepticism that leads to solipsism or nihilism is simply labeled "trite." And the first two parts, by demolishing various forms of "improper" and useless skepticism, lay the groundwork for the usefulness and durability of a mitigated skepticism outlined in the third part of the essay. When we consider the narrow limitations of any inquiry, Hume suggests, we cannot hope for too much since we do not have the means to achieve those hopes; nor should we expect too little since the world is not chaotic.

The kind of skepticism that Hume advocates is often Pyrrhonistic, but it fixes boundaries upon human inquiries. It is, as numerous commentators have observed, a species of naturalism. Though questioning the evidence offered in support of a theory demonstrating the uniformity of nature, Hume found himself believing in the uniformity of nature. He cannot accept as fact what his experience does not teach him. Newton observed that the inductive method of reasoning could never produce certainty, but that, as methodology, it was the best we had.[12] Hume's skepticism accepts the truth of his proposition, "Whatever *is* may *not* be"; and it attempts to cope with the divergent experience of human nature with a full awareness of that handicap.

Although perhaps not representative, the last paragraph of the first *Enquiry* is deservedly the most famous. In historical context, it is not so dashing as it seems; for the "school metaphysics" that Hume berates had long ago passed on to its reward.[13] Yet its rhetoric at least gives us a clue to Hume's attitude toward a priori theorizing and empty speculation. It can easily bear requoting: "When we run over libraries, persuaded of these principles, what havoc must we make? If we take in our hand any volume; of divinity or school metaphysics, for instance; let us ask, *Does it contain any abstract reasoning concerning quantity or number.* No. *Does it contain any experimental reasoning concerning matter of fact and existence?* No. Commit it then to the flames: For it can contain nothing but sophistry and illusion." (*Works*, IV, 135; *ECHU*, 158).

II *The Principles of Morals: Semantics and Secularism*

Hume's strategy in the *Enquiry concerning the Principles of Morals* is indeed hopeful: to attempt the same reformation in ethics as Newton had done in "natural philosophy," and to reject any system of ethics not established by facts or observation. The results are certainly different from those of previous ethical systems. Hume's ethic is completely secular, more so than those of Spinoza, Bayle, Montaigne, Hobbes, or Francis Hutcheson. Hume's secularism is thus not unique, but it is different from the secularism of Hutcheson's ethic, to take one of Hume's contemporaries as an example. Hutcheson's secular ethic operates within human limits and limitations, but it relates moral activity to the Deity and speculates about the role of the Deity in moral decisions, something Hume conspicuously avoided.

Hume's methodology is deceptively simple. By close observation of noteworthy human transactions, he plans to isolate whatever mental qualities account for personal merit. He attends to the terminology applied in moral judgments in order to discover what

similarities in criteria exist. Our language makes rhetoric an inescapable part of any system of ethics since many words are inextricably associated with specific sets of ideas about morality. To gain
proper perspective, Hume adds a historical dimension to his approach. Activities or qualities of the mind which excite general
approbation are called "virtuous"; activities or qualities of the
mind which are blamed or censured are in general termed "vicious." [14] Hume plans to follow the generally reliable method of
experimental reasoning and to infer general maxims from se-
quences of particular instances. The best method for establishing
a system of ethics is first to discover what human interchanges
have been accounted ethical. Hume's procedure involves an attack on one of the most common principles in the eighteenth century for ethical systems, self-love.[15]

In all editions of the second *Enquiry* which appeared during
Hume's lifetime, the second section, "Of Benevolence," was first
devoted to a discussion of self-love. In the authoritative edition of
1777, however, the section on self-love was relegated to an appendix, where it has gone unnoticed by almost all of Hume's commentators. Since the various ideas suggested by the concept "self-
love" provided the seventeenth and eighteenth centuries with
fruitful means of unifying and formulating ethical systems,
Hume's discussion of self-love is of more than cursory interest.
Moreover, much of what Hume says about self-love in the relocated part of Section II prepares the reader for his inquiry into
the origin of moral principles. Hume's ethical postulates and assertions cannot be fully understood without understanding his attitude toward and his concept of self-love. For that reason, I
should like to devote this section primarily to an account of
Hume's reflections upon self-love.

The relocated section does not constitute the totality of Hume's
views on self-love, for he mentions or discusses the concept in the
Treatise, in his essays, in the *History of England,* and in the *Dialogues concerning Natural Religion.* The second *Enquiry* presented his most sustained consideration. Hume begins by noticing
the existence of a principle asserting that benevolence, friendship,
public spirit, and other like virtues are not what they seem. Hume,
who refuses to accept this idea, makes several ad hominem observations about the kind of "heart" to be found in the enunciator of
such views. Another view holds that no passions are disinterested,

that friendship is an extension or outlet for self-love: regardless of our putative motives, the ultimate motive must be self-love.

In spite of this insistence upon self-love as the source of seeming benevolence, the philosophers who advocated some kind of self-love as the ultimate ethical doctrine were themselves friendly and generous (for example, Epicurus, Atticus, and Horace; Hobbes and Locke). An Epicurean or Hobbesean admitted the existence of friendship in the world, and Hume cannot, as a matter of rhetoric and logic, accept the attempt to call it another form of self-love. Hume admires results: he esteems the man whose self-love leads him into acts of charity or benevolence, regardless of the assignment others make of his motives. Distinguishing between two kinds of benevolence (general and particular), Hume argues that both kinds must exist in human nature. Any resolution of them into some "nice consideration of self-love" is more curious than important. Hume remarks, ironically, that all attempts to prove benevolence, for example, to be something other than it is (that is, to be self-love) have been fruitless; such attempts proceed from the love of simplicity, "which has been the source of much false reasoning in philosophy" (*Works*, IV, 269; *ECPM*, 116).

An ethical system based on self-love is attractive, Hume continues, because it accounts for the origin of benevolence in selfishness. As we inquire about the origin of our passions, we do not suppose that they came from the least obvious and least familiar causes. The more intricate and refined a system is, the more we are apt to suspect it. By applying Occam's razor to elaborate theories dependent upon self-love to explain human motives, Hume argues that we ought always to assume that the simplest and most obvious cause for the operation of the passions is correct. He points out that animals show kindness to other animals and to humans; yet we do not impute their motives to self-love. Surely we can be as charitable toward human beings as we are toward animals. Parental devotion, Hume says, cannot be accounted for by self-love. The most important objection Hume makes is metalinguistic. Hume asks why we have a word like "gratitude" if it is to have no meaning or reality, if we are to have no methodology for knowing what the word means. If we are to consider gratitude as only disguised self-love, then we ought indeed to reduce all human acts to species of self-love. Not even the advocates of an

ethical system based on self-love have adopted this procedure, as
Hume points out; and they have certainly not practiced it.

Returning to his observation about the great dangers of simplicity in philosophical reasoning, Hume observes that the hypothesis
allowing the existence of disinterested benevolence is simpler than
one asserting self-love. To make self-love the source of all charity
is to confound and needlessly to complicate inquiries into the
principles of morals. In addition, certain passions, like the love of
fame, must precede self-love; if we seek fame, we must first obtain
it before our self-love can allow us to enjoy it. To distinguish between self-enjoyment and self-love is necessary if we are to comprehend moral acts. Self-love cannot explain all of our actions and
reactions: "If I have no vanity, I take no delight in praise: If I be
void of ambition, power gives me no enjoyment: If I be not
angry, the punishment of an adversary is totally indifferent to me"
(*Works*, IV, 271; *ECPM*, 118). Without experience to teach us
the difference between pain and pleasure, self-love could exert no
influence on us. Some inclinations or appetites must exist prior to
whatever self-love may arise in an individual; otherwise nothing
would call it forth.

Hume finally appeals to the "original frame of our temper" to
establish the possibility of "real" benevolence and friendship. Reason and experience accord more with the attribution of benevolence and friendship to a natural propensity on the part of an
individual than they do with self-love. Self-enjoyment may result
from the pleasure we have in benevolence, but self-enjoyment and
self-love are not identical. Indeed, Hume says, the passion of
anger may carry us into undesirable pursuits; and self-love could
do little to restrain our vindictiveness. Philosophy can at least permit humanity and friendship the same privileges ascribed to en-
mity and resentment. Human nature is not capable of being explained by an appeal to some abstract universal principle. At the
risk of an anachronism, I should say that Hume finds masochistic
the practice of attributing only evil passions and malign sentiments to human beings. And a projection of individualized consciousness is not sufficient for inquiry into the reasons for the principles of morals.

Why Hume relegated this part of Section II to an appendix can
only be conjectured. Generally speaking, he viewed self-love as
one of the least admirable of human passions, although he did not

find it so opprobrious as other vices; yet the concept is essential in his ethical system. The difficulty with self-love as an ethical concept is that it usually involves a "ruling passion" theory of ethics—one Hume specifically abjured as the basis of ethics. On several occasions he said that human behavior could not be explained by appeal to some passion or principle to account for the totality of ethical conduct. None of the ideas or concepts—such as "benevolence," "justice," or "utility," which Hume discusses in the *Enquiry concerning the Principles of Morals*—is sufficient in itself to form or to animate a theory of ethics; nor does he intend that one of them should be sufficient.

For convenience, I have been referring to Hume's "system of ethics" and its formation; but to credit Hume with a system of ethics is perhaps misleading. As the title indicates, Hume is inquiring into the principles of morals, an activity that is different from erecting a system of morals. Hume's general conclusions, which will seem simple-minded to those unfamiliar with the history of ethical speculation, are not likely to shock or even to enlighten the modern mind. His ethic is primarily descriptive, not prescriptive; and thus it has neither the rhetoric nor the sweeping autonomy of systems of ethics. Instead of the imperative sentences that we might expect from a discussion of morality, Hume's are chiefly declarative. I hasten to add that he commits himself by implication to a traditional ethical position. His language clearly implies what qualities he finds virtuous and what vicious.

The key to Hume's moral outlook is probably best found in Section V, "Why Utility Pleases." The sections after it discuss qualities useful and agreeable to ourselves and to others, indicating the extent to which Hume emphasizes the importance of utility in moral acts. "Why Utility Pleases" is a more important section than the three following ones because Hume seeks in it to explain rather than to enumerate the considerations of ethics. Interestingly enough, Hume is concerned in this section to demonstrate the inadequacy of self-love as a concept sufficient to explain all action. This undertaking reinforced Bishop Butler's answer to theories of ethics denying the possibility of disinterested moral action.[16]

To give utility the same praise that we would give any social virtue would seem "natural" in ethical inquiry; but, Hume notes, philosophers have not often done so because of the difficulty of accounting for the origin of usefulness as an ethical criterion. Suggesting that confusion of the two notions of utility has been one of the reasons for this difficulty, Hume distinguishes between utility which lends virtue to its owner and utility in an inanimate object. Social virtues naturally recommend themselves to the mind, prior to admonitions or education. The public utility of these virtues causes them to be considered meritorious, and the ends these virtues promote please either from selfish interests (self-love) or from generosity and humanity. Hume again asserts that moral systems cannot be derived from or based on concepts of self-love; to allege that benevolence and humanity are only forms of modified self-love is to forsake linguistic accuracy for a generalization supporting the tradition of man's innate sinfulness. Theories of self-love cannot account sufficiently for the agreeableness and pleasure of usefulness. The approbation accorded usefulness is universal and not particular; it cannot be reconciled with a denial of the possibility of disinterested moral action.

Hume does admit, however, that self-love is a forceful and extensive principle in human nature and that philosophers who sought to account for all activity in its terms can perhaps be excused for their shortsightedness. Because the interests of the individual seem coextensive with those of his society, other philosophers enforced a unity upon moral activity that did not, in fact, exist. To support his argument on strictly empirical grounds, Hume marshals category after category of examples which cannot be sufficiently justified by a self-love theory of ethics. Considering the subject on both a priori and a posteriori grounds, Hume argues against the oversimplification of ethics into theories of self-interest and self-love. What else, he asks, but a general goodwill towards one's fellow creatures could account for utilitarian value that disinterested spectators assign to social virtue? In qualities that are useful to ourselves, such as efficiency in the dispatch of our business, self-love does not and cannot account for the pleasure which that quality in us would give to other people; but any number of us are pleased to observe a man who does his job well. Even those qualities that are pleasing solely to us cannot be always resolved into self-love. Agility of mind is both useful and pleasant to ourselves, but it was not created by our self-love. In short, the usefulness of these pleasing qualities enlarges our capacity for understanding ourselves and others better than we otherwise would.

The purpose of ethics is to inquire into the criteria for determining good and bad actions in order to ascertain whatever personal merit any individual has. Neither reason nor sentiment is sufficient in and of itself to arrive at correct moral equations. For Hume, personal merit "consists altogether in the possession of mental qualities, *useful* or *agreeable* to the *person himself* or to *others*" (*Works*, IV, 245; *ECPM*, 89). While philosophers may have disputed this activist definition of personal merit (or virtue), common life, where most moral transactions take place, implicitly accepts and acts upon those principles. Certain qualities, like the "monkish virtues" of "celibacy, fasting, penance, mortification, self-denial, humility, silence, solitude" are always rejected by "sensible" men because they have no function, they are not valuable to society, and they usually render their owner unfit for human intercourse. With this observation, Hume explicitly rejects both the ascetic and the Puritan tradition in ethics; in fact, he labels these ascetic qualities "vices."

In coming to a conclusion about the proper subject matter of morals, Hume excludes such passions as avarice, ambition, and vanity from the account of the origin of morals. Those passions are incorrectly thought to be forms of self-love, but Hume does not think they can account for the formation of moral sentiments. Morality must be dependent upon a universal propensity in mankind to agree about some object or person deserving approval. Since the sentiment of humanity is more widespread than that of self-love, self-love cannot be the foundation of morality. The concern of morality is general principles; morality does not assert or propound a ruling passion that governs all men regardless of what they think.

In the "Conclusion," Hume articulates the essential differences between the language of self-love and that of ordinary moral transactions. By qualifying nouns with a possessive adjective (e.g., *his* rival), a man relates the events of his experience specifically to himself and not to the generality of mankind. To describe a man as "odious" or "depraved," however, is to expect the concurrence of one's listeners, or, anyway, not to be astonished at any disagreement. The language of ethics, Hume implies, is amenable to the kind of experience and verification that one applies in "natural philosophy" or history. Its judgments are understood because they are universal, and men throughout history experience much the same sentiment or passion upon hearing lies or viewing cruelty.[17] Because human emotions and affections share a number of similarities in all human beings, the same linguistic criteria for determining a useful chair could be applied to determining a courageous decision.

Hume insists upon a dichotomy between what we may call "private moral experiences" and "public moral activities." General sentiments, not private passions, of humanity are the origin of morals. The difference is great: "Whatever conduct gains my approbation, by touching my humanity, procures also the applause of all mankind, by affecting the same principle in them: But what serves my avarice or ambition pleases these passions in me alone, and affects not the avarice and ambition of the rest of mankind" (*Works*, IV, 249; *ECPM*, 94). Language is formed on the vast distinction between these two species of sentiment. Specific manifestations of self-love are controlled and modified by the universal principles which have been incorporated into the sum and substance of our language. What Hume calls "benevolent concern for others" is not, of course, equally diffused in all men. And the objects of that concern may well vary since education or reason directs concern toward specific people. Yet every quality of the mind useful or agreeable to its owner or to others also renders pleasure to the generality of mankind and is usually thought meritorious.

These views of Hume's here outlined may seem facile, even naïve, to the modern reader. So far as I can tell, they did not to the eighteenth-century reader; for none of the eighteenth-century reviews or discussions of the *Enquiry concerning the Principles of Morals* which I have examined has charged Hume with such. The reason may be attributable to the latent skepticism, which becomes straightforward in the last part of Hume's conclusion, of the second *Enquiry*. Confessing that he cannot at present imagine any forcible objections to his contention that personal merit is made up of the utility or agreeableness of personal qualities, he does realize the probability of error. The confusion and errors resulting from what was thought precision in measuring the bulk of the earth and the order of the universe are sufficient examples. His hypothesis, while seeming so obvious, must, to the skeptical mind, invite dispute and correction; otherwise it would long ago have been unanimously accepted. Thus, Hume ironically suggests that men's certitudes are likely to fool no one but themselves.

This skepticism leads Hume into a consideration of one's obligation or duty to promote virtue and to discourage vice. And the skeptic asks what hope can we have of convincing mankind to accept the rigorous and austere ethic that grows out of the sentiments of all mankind. The advantage of the principles Hume has posited lies in their usefulness to the individual. Fame and honor, even ingenuity and politeness, are qualities no one would willingly forego, if one is educated. The opposition of selfish and social sentiments is no more accurate than the opposition of selfishness and vanity, of selfishness and ambition. Before self-love can direct our energies and passions, we must have already engaged our affections, our natural propensities. If we wish the approbation of our fellow men, we can do no less than exemplify the virtues that language has traditionally defined. Giving all possible credit to vice, we would not find it more rewarding than the practice of virtue with whatever view to self-interest we may have. And we will discover that the principles of morals are general guides, not autonomous rules. The wise man knows the exceptions to the general rules and uses them judiciously.

Reason impels man to accept the moral principles described by our language. If he does not, if he cannot find reason for seeking and promoting personal merit, then, Hume skeptically concludes, he is unlikely to be convinced by any argument. A man who does not understand the general sentiments of mankind or the language in which morality is couched is beyond the reach of human communication.

In this discussion, I have hoped to enforce two ideas about Hume's method and purpose in the *Enquiry concerning the Principles of Morals*. First, I think it is clear that Hume wished to lay to rest forever the notion that all acts were the product of self-love, that the narcissistic element in man was too strong to include the possibility of disinterested moral action. Second, he found in the forms of language the structure of ethics, and he tried to show the inescapable interconnections between discourses about ethics and the language used to make those discourses. To reformulate ethics along these lines precluded any attempt to separate the business of ethics from that of everyday life. In addition, these guidelines provided an ethic whose authority was secular, not sacred, and was consequently more universal than any ethic derived from religious precepts. No one will argue that Hume's inquiry is perfect as an attempt to establish the principles of morals, but we can say of it, as Dr. Johnson said of his *Dictionary*, "In this work, when it shall be found that much is omitted, let it not be forgotten that much likewise is performed. . . ."

CHAPTER 5

Hume as Historian

I *The* History of England: *Background and Methodology*

A S early as 1745, Hume was making plans to write a history of England; and for the next decade he collected facts, information, and ideas for this history. Although the first volume of his *History of England* was not published until 1754, and the second volume in 1757, Hume was nevertheless planning, in the 1740's, what kind of history he would write.[1] In the surviving manuscript notes for his history, we can see that Hume made careful outlines of certain portions of English history, apparently trying to familiarize himself with the material to be assimilated and the sources necessary for that assimilation.[2]

To write a history of England was no easy task, although several people, as we have seen (in Chapter 1), had attempted either a comprehensive or a selective history of England. While Hume's history is not exactly comprehensive, it attempted to do more than any of his predecessors had done. Hume's most important predecessor was Rapin-Thoyras, and the defects of his history of England were not always outweighed by its achievements. Hume set for himself, then, one of the most important tasks of any writer in the eighteenth century: to write a readable and intelligent history of England, free of fractious partisanship, impartial where possible, judicious even when unnecessary.

To attempt to be fair and impartial is, of course, the intention if not the claim of most authors. Yet some of the difficulties attendant upon writing a complete history of England were not unknown to Hume's contemporaries. James Ralph's exhausting[3] *History of England,* covering the years 1688 to 1702, had noted in its introductory review of the Restoration some of the imponderables of writing history. Ralph points out the vagaries of writing about events when they are not yet history, and the importance, once they are past, of achieving a proper perspective for viewing them.

Unfortunately, Ralph observes, all Englishmen are members of some party or faction; because they share common creeds, to judge the past virtues or sins of their party or faction may be very painful or even impossible. "Thus," Ralph says, "should an *Historian* arise, who had Application to collect the best Materials, Capacity to comprehend, and Skill to digest them, Genius to animate his Work, and Integrity and Resolution so to decide upon every Character and every Fact, as Equity should prompt, as Truth should authorise, instead of making Converts, by the honest Exercise of his Talents, he would possibly make Enemies; and all the *Sore* among the *Living* would clamour in Behalf of the *guilty Dead*." [4]

In Ralph's estimation, the perils of writing history lie more with the putative historian than with the frequent irreconcilability of facts and events. He is nonetheless hopeful: "But should so valuable a Man ever arise among us, I hope he would venture upon the Task, however difficult and discouraging, of reducing our shapeless Annals into Form and Comeliness, with a Spirit superior to any such ungrateful Consequence." [5] Although neither man may have known the other, James Ralph outlined in 1744 the kind of historian Hume hoped to be. Ralph's history covered, of course, periods that Hume did not cover, but which, in 1763, he thought of covering; and he sought to obtain Ralph's materials for that purpose. To his publisher, Andrew Millar, he wrote, "I am told, that Mr. Ralph is dead, who had certainly made a large Collection of Books and Pamphlets for his Work. I should be glad to know into whose hands they are fallen, and would purchase them, if they could be got at a reasonable Price" (*HL*, I, 382). If nothing else, Hume admired the scholarship that went into Ralph's work. I do not know if Hume was aware of Ralph's work when he began the actual writing of his own history of England; but that he should not seems unlikely in view of his wide reading and his lengthy preparation for his *History of England*. He may have decided to omit a history of the periods after the "Glorious Revolution" since Ralph had already covered them and since Hume was not inclined to write a history of his own times.

Hume did agree with Ralph's general sentiments about the problems of writing history and of being a historian. Before undertaking the task, he thought carefully about the problems with which he would be faced. Since no one before him had at-

tempted the kind of history of England that Hume wished to
write, he had no model to follow; but he did have some general
ideas about the form and function of a history.

As we have seen in Chapter 1, in a letter of Hume's to John
Clephane, he confided that he was engaged upon a project which
would keep him busy for several years, his *History of England:*

My friends flatter me (by this I mean that they don't flatter me), that
I have succeeded. You know that there is no post of honour in the
English Parnassus more vacant than that of History. Style, judgement,
impartiality, care—everything is wanting to our historians; and even
Rapin, during this latter period, is extremely deficient. I make my work
very concise, after the manner of the Ancients. It divides into three
very moderate volumes; one to end with the death of Charles the First;
the second at the Revolution; the third at the Accession [Hanover], for
I dare come no nearer to the present times. The work will neither please
the Duke of Bedford nor James Fraser; but I hope it will please you
and posterity.   Κτῆμα εἰς ἀεί   ["A possession for all times"]. (*HL*, I,
170–71)

Actually, the projected third volume mentioned in this letter
was never attempted, for Hume only took his history up through
1689. At this time, Hume had apparently planned to write no
more than the history of the Stuarts, but the first two volumes
mentioned here became the last two volumes of the completed
history. The conclusion of the above letter indicates to what extent Hume thought he was being impartial since John, fourth
Duke of Bedford, exemplified everything that Whigs stood for,
while James Fraser was an enthusiastic Jacobite.[6] Thus, before
the *History of England* was published, Hume had hoped that it
would please the judicious and would be "a possession for all
time," as he quoted Thucydides.

Even after protests were raised about Hume's alleged political
bias, he still thought himself moderate. John Clephane received
another letter from Hume after the first volume of the *History* was
published, where Hume articulated, in a famous passage, part of
his methodology: "My views of *things* are more conformable to
Whig principles; my representations of *persons* to Tory prejudices" (*HL*, I, 237). Finding himself numbered among the Tories
more often than among the Whigs was ample proof, he added, of
men's higher regard for persons rather than things. Yet Hume

thought this regard was as it should be, for he had no wish to write a history consisting only of fact, fact, fact.

To avoid the dullness and sterility of history as fact, fact, fact is not, however, to write a history that is fantasy, fantasy, fantasy. Writing a history of anything requires that one have, obviously, some conception of history, some plan of organizing materials, and some discretion in the choice of representative events. We may never be sure what Hume's concept of history was, nor can we isolate all of his intentions in writing a history of England. But we can recreate, from various scattered comments, some idea of the form and function of history as Hume conceived it. The presentation of historical facts and events necessarily involves discrimination among one's sources. The discriminations and judgments made about the sources and presentation create the perspective from which a history is written.

In outlining Hume's concept of history, we could turn first to an essay that appeared in 1741, "Of the Study of History." This essay appeared in all editions of Hume's essays through 1760, but it was withdrawn as another of the essays Hume thought "too frivolous," from the edition of the *Essays and Treatises on Several Subjects* published in 1764. Although not as weighty as some of his other essays, it does contain some helpful observations. In the essay, Hume joshingly asserts that the study of history recommends itself to the female sex as suited for their education and instruction more so than the usual books of amusement or instruction. History will convey to them two important truths: (1) that the male sex is not so perfect as they imagine, and (2) that love is not the sole governing passion of men and is often overcome by other passions. Hume continues in this vein for two paragraphs and then admits his ironic raillery. Yet his suggestions, he alleges, are not without merit; for history is indeed an agreeable entertainment because it transports the mind to other cultures and other societies. A knowledge of history is necessary for the well-educated man or woman, and ignorance of historical facts is unpardonable in a person pretending to erudition. To these advantages, Hume adds history's capacity for introducing one to new realms of inquiry; moreover, it can promote virtue without leading to the difficulties poetry might entail.

While Hume began his essay frivolously, he suggests in its last paragraph two of the important functions of history. Because a historian is, says Hume, unlike the poet, and must represent passions in all their glory or iniquity, he inculcates a sense of virtue. He must be judicious, but he is not always impartial; he may err in his judgment of particular persons, but he must not do so in representing vice and virtue in their proper perspectives. Hume's observations about the philosopher's contemplation of history are even more instructive. Taking an abstract view of men, manners, and things, the philosopher is often unmoved by the general sentiments of human nature. Because he does not enter into that which he contemplates, he often does not feel the difference between vice and virtue. That which is temporally distant loses much of its humanity when viewed from a philosophic standpoint. The study of history, Hume continues, prevents this distortion by mediating between the extremes (1) of indifference to virtue or vice and (2) of atrophy of natural sentiments. Writers of history, as well as the readers, respond to instances of vice or virtue since they must pay attention to characters and events. The temporal distance from the characters or events described usually precludes any interest on the part of the narrator or reader, but it encourages correct moral or political judgments.

We saw in Chapter 2 some of the epistemological problems with which the reader or the chronicler of history is confronted. The greatest epistemological problem that confronted any historian, Hume no less than his predecessors, was that of the reliability of the data from which the history was to be constructed. As years pass and as men become more and more removed from the important events of history, the evidence for their occurrence becomes harder to verify. Hume's solution to the difficulty, first raised in the *Treatise,* was neither original nor imaginative. He relied upon the metaphor of the "chain of argument" to suggest the continuity that is somehow preserved in any narrative, spoken or written, of historical events. He invokes the doctrine of "common sense" to suggest that few will doubt that a man such as Julius Caesar ever existed. As a matter of expedience, Hume is right: few will ever doubt that Julius Caesar existed. Important events and men are testified to in many documents as well as by tradition. But, Hume points out, the events and men of lesser importance do not share in this extensiveness. Given a similarity in the reports of one historical occurrence, the historian can safely include it as "fact" in his composition. What is the historian to do, however, when the reports conflict or seem otherwise unreliable?

Hume's method for dealing with such instances is simple. The limits of experience prevent absolute assertions about the truth-value of any proposition. Moreover, the propositions of history are not the same as those about scientific facts, which are capable of re-verification. To determine the truth-value of historical propositions, the historian must confine the evidence to the context in which they appear. Historical propositions are subject to means of verification different from the procedure for other propositions. In the *Treatise*, as noted above, Hume mentioned two admittedly unoriginal guides to determining the truth-value of historical propositions. In writing the *History of England*, he employed a methodology consistent with his assertions about the principles of human nature. (This is not to say that Hume's *History* is "philosophical," although one might easily come to read it with that preconception.[7]) The methodology exhibits Hume's willingness to judge the validity or reliability of the reports from which he composed his history.

An example of this methodology can be found in the *History*, in Chapter 2, in which Hume covers the period from 827 through 978. In discussing Anglo-Saxon King Edgar, he relies upon a number of documents spelling out the administrative details of his reign. He notes some disagreement among Scottish historians about the allegiance of the Scottish king, Kenneth III, to Edgar. Hume ignores these problems and points to the primary way in which Edgar maintained authority: by cultivating the monks and others who, by pretending to superior sanctity and purity, had more influence with the people than any other group. When the union of crown and church proved to be successful, Edgar exploited it by condemning the secular clergy. The monks were enjoined to rid the monasteries of reprobates and backsliders, which they did. Yet Hume is appropriately skeptical about the evidence offered to support the allegations against the secular clergy:

We may remark, that the declamations against the secular clergy are, both here and in all the historians, conveyed in general terms; and as that order of men are commonly restrained by the decency of their character, [not to mention superior motives,] it is difficult to believe that the complaints against their dissolute manners could be so universally just as is pretended. It is more probable that the monks paid

court to the populace by an affected austerity of life; and representing
the most innocent liberties, taken by the other clergy as great and
unpardonable enormities, thereby prepared the way for the encrease
of their own power and influence. (*History*, I, Chapter II, 120–21
[passage in brackets omitted from Hume's last revised edition].)

The "innocent liberties" to which Hume refers include gaming,
hunting, singing, dancing, and living with one's wife—"liberties"
denied the regular clergy.

The passage omitted from the last revised edition of the *History*
contains, I think, the clue to Hume's methodology in narrating
history where the facts are scarce or contradictory. He suspects
any generalization contrary to ordinary experience and custom.
Having no firsthand, reliable accounts of various events, Hume
imposes upon the popular, yet questionable, generalizations some
of his ideas about the mechanics of human nature. The limits of
historical truth and reliability are fixed by the implications of
Hume's moral and epistemological presumptions. Within this
framework, Hume can and does make certain assertions about
evidence he thinks untrustworthy. (I think we can agree that any
assertion about men's motives must, as a matter of logic, influence
the historian's conclusions.)

Hume remarks, for example, that the members of the secular
clergy were of decent character and entered into their work with
motives superior to those of the regular clergy (or so Hume would
seem to imply). Thus, one part of Hume's methodology in writing
his history involves his ideas about men's motives in choosing X
rather than Y. The limitless implications of this methodology are
restrained by Hume's reluctance to substitute one questionable
generalization for another and by his inclination to be suspicious
of the professionally pious. While the eighteenth-century reader
may have been incensed at the implications of Hume's remarks
about the monks' affectations, he might, with better reason, have
questioned Hume's mixture of evidence. What Hume says about
the reasons for the monks' aversion to the secular clergy is acceptable, but we might very well wonder about the way in which the
conclusion was reached.

In short, Hume distrusts generalized accounts of specific events.
Lacking historical evidence, he tries to explain what *might* have
happened in terms of the principles of human nature. This expla-

nation we might expect of Hume, whose first interest was philosophy. One twentieth-century commentator remarked of the philosophy in the *History* that "It is only when the *History of England* is read with a critical eye that the immense amount of thought involved in it becomes apparent, and the reader realizes that what seemed to be a simple, straightforward narrative of fact is really a highly polished and skilfully articulated philosophy of history. Moreover, the philosophy is so subtly insinuated into the texture of the work, so artistically blended with it, that the task of effecting a separation is by no means easy." [8] While I do not think we can find specific correlations between the ideas in the *History of England* and Hume's ethical and metaphysical positions, we can safely assume that his philosophical inclinations predisposed him to treat the uncertain in history the same way in which he treated it in philosophy. He specifically admits to this procedure in discussing Queen Elizabeth's reign: "Whoever enlarges his view, and reflects on the situations, will remark the necessary progress of human affairs, and the operation of those principles which are inherent in human nature" (*History*, V, Chapter XXXVIII, 21).

When the facts are too few or too general, the historian fills in what he can with observations based upon his particular insight into human nature. What is he to do when the facts are many? Hume addressed himself to this problem in opening his discussion of Henry III, with the following observation: "Most sciences, in proportion as they increase and improve, invent methods by which they facilitate their reasonings; and, employing general theorems, are enabled to comprehend, in a few propositions, a great number of inferences and conclusions. History also, being a collection of facts which are multiplying without end, is obliged to adopt such arts of abridgment, to retain the more material events, and to drop all the minute circumstances, which are only interesting during the time, or the persons engaged in the transaction" (*History*, II, Chapter XII, 143). Hume then remarks that this truth is nowhere more evident than in the reign of Henry III: no mortal would be patient enough to read all the trivia and frivolities by which the weaknesses of "so mean a prince as Henry" were distinguished.

We might object to this procedure, as Professor J. B. Black did,[9] by seeing in it a subjective interpretation of history, which would discourage historical research by assuming that all facts are

not potentially valuable. Yet we must remember that Hume was
writing what was really the first successful history of England,
and he foresaw these difficulties. The histories of others had often
failed simply because they crammed too much minutiae into their
narratives, and Ralph's history was a good example of this practice. Hume's history was indeed different in its selectivity, and
part of his methodology involved a wish to have his *History of
England* be a popular success. The view articulated above represents Hume's attempts to cope both with the vastness of English
history and its relative importance. Events of interest only to the
professional student of history could be safely omitted if no injus-
tice were done to the events that actually shaped men's lives. For
convenience, I have suggested that Hume's *History* was comprehensive; perhaps it would be more exact to say that Hume wanted
his *History* to be both comprehensible and comprehending. He
wanted it to appeal to the average intelligent reader of his time;
he wanted to exhibit both a grasp of the important affairs of state
and an ability to see them in the proper perspective; and he
wanted this perspective to inculcate certain moral attitudes.

This desire to limit the scope of a historical discussion, as well
as the physical size of the volumes, is expressed in Hume's letter to
the historian William Robertson. Robertson's *History of Scotland*
appeared January 29, 1759; Hume read it and made several comments about the style and the methodology. Having finished one
history, Robertson was looking for the subject of another and apparently wrote to Hume for some suggestions. Hume pointed out
the difficulties and the advantages of ancient Greek history and
then mentioned Thomas Leland's *History of the Life and Reign of
Philip, King of Macedon* (1758): "There is one Dr Leland, who
has lately wrote the Life of Philip of Macedon, which is one of the
best Periods: The Book, they tell me, is perfectly well wrote; yet it
has had such small Sale, & has so little excited the Attention of the
Public, that the Author has Reason to think his Labour thrown
away. I have not read the Book; but by the Size, I should judge it
to be too particular. It is a pretty large Quarto; I think a Book of
that Size sufficient for the whole History of Greece till the Death
of Philip . . ." (*NHL*, 48). While neither the modern historian
nor the modern reader may approve of this arbitrary limit, Hume's
reasons seem justifiable in his own terms. He did not "use" his
History to preach to his readers, but he did impose arbitrary limits

on its narration in order to appeal to as many readers as possible. The preceding statements suggest that Hume was interested only in those periods of British history which had some profound effect on the course of British civilization. And, indeed, those periods received the most attention, as Hume himself realized. He remarked in the first chapter (actually, one of the last parts of the *History* to be written) that

Ingenious men, possessed of leisure, are apt to push their researches beyond the period in which literary monuments are framed or preserved; without reflecting, that the history of past events is immediately lost or disfigured when entrusted to memory and oral tradition, and that the adventures of barbarous nations, even if they were recorded, could afford little or no entertainment to men born in a more cultivated age. The convulsions of a civilized state usually compose the most instructive and most interesting part of its history; but the sudden, violent, and unprepared revolutions incident to Barbarians, are so much guided by caprice and terminate so often in cruelty, that they disgust us by the uniformity of their appearance; and it is rather fortunate for letters that they are buried in silence and oblivion. (*History*, I, Chapter I, 1–2)

Hume's history is, he says, devoted to the ways in which civilization is advanced and not to the fables and traditions associated with a body of people. Hume's chief interest in writing history lies in the representation of the various forces—moral, political, and economic—which shaped the progress of British civilization and which improved political stability. The result was, he hoped, a "more full narration for those times when the truth is both so well ascertained and so complete as to promise entertainment and instruction to the reader" (*History*, I, Chapter I, 2).

Hume thus accepted as two of his many guidelines two cherished criteria of Renaissance critics: the entertainment and instruction of readers. History's value could be both hedonistic and utilitarian. Hume wanted to bring into proper focus all the events which contributed to the formation of civilized manners in Great Britain. He was admittedly selective when incorporating facts into his history, but he avoided what he would have called the "vulgar error" of ignoring facts that contravened the instructiveness of his examples. This methodology, faulty in several ways to the modern historian, led Hume into various judgments about the events or

characters in his narration. Because of his selectivity and because
of the wish to instruct and to entertain—among other reasons—
Hume permitted his *History of England* to display some of his
philosophical positions, political attitudes, and moral judgments.

II   *The* History of England: *Principles in Retrospect*

To observe that we can find in a historical work the presupposi-
tions and principles of the author is hardly astonishing. No one
doubts that the beliefs and opinions of an author influence or
affect his writing in one way or another. He can be bitterly polemical, as Bishop William Warburton was, without realizing just
how far from the mainstream of ideas he is. To the eyes of someone like Warburton the most extravagant statements may seem
too obvious for clarification; certain principles become so much a
part of the writer's personality, as well as the rhetoric with which
one expresses oneself, that they seem indistinguishable from the
objects of perception. In contrast, another author may be keenly
aware that his opinions, prejudices, and ideas are uncommon and,
often, unacceptable. Attempting to avoid fractious partisanship,
this author over-compensates for his ideas and may completely
obliterate them. He goes out of his way to be fair to the opposition, with the result that he sometimes appears to be numbered
among those whom he opposes. To tread the thin line between
these two extremes is a cliché every writer invokes, and Hume, as
we have seen, invoked it. As Hume himself tells us in his autobiography, his *History* had the misfortune of both extremes. Because he bent over backwards to be fair to policies and people not
meeting his approval, he was accused of being one of them; because of his reputation as a dangerous free-thinker, he was accused of injecting atheism into his work.

To find Hume's opinions and judgments about events and
people in the *History of England* requires little effort. What distinguishes them at once from his philosophical speculations and
reasoning is the rhetoric. Hume is nowhere *less* skeptical about
the efficacy of moral judgments, for example, than in the *History
of England*. These judgments are not fixed by either the rhetoric
or the logic that we discover in his abstract contemplations about
the principles of morals, politics, or economics. It was, of course,
the prerogative of the eighteenth-century writer to indulge himself often in moral judgments, regardless of the work under con-

sideration. After all, what is the purpose of "moral science"? No one can read Dr. Johnson without being aware that moral attitudes and prescriptions affix themselves most firmly to almost all of his literary principles. In fact, Dr. Johnson would probably have approved of most of Hume's moral and political judgments in the *History of England*, if he had read it.[10] While Hume is not so openly moralistic as Dr. Johnson—and he had of course displeased Johnson with his skeptical inquiries into the principles of religion and morality—his moral judgments could easily coincide with Johnson's, except when Hume's judgments were made as a result of what Hume considered an abuse of religious power.

Writing of the early Anglo-Saxon kings, Hume discovered innumerable abuses of religious power, most of which resulted from the imposition of clerical authority in secular matters. The misfortunes of King Edwy illustrate the abuses. Hume narrates Edwy's passion for Princess Elgiva, whose "softer pleasures" led to their being discovered, apparently, *in flagrante delicto*. Dunstan, the Abbott of Glastenbury, and Odo, the Archbishop of Canterbury, hoped to improve their political position by this opportunity; but Edwy, who managed to reverse his misfortune, succeeded in banishing Dunstan. During Dunstan's absence, however, his cabal was active; and it succeeded in torturing and banishing Elgiva. When she attempted to return, Odo had her murdered; with the return of Dunstan, Odo instituted a revolt against the King, who was excommunicated. The death of Edwy passed the crown to his brother Edgar. In discussing the peaceful reign of Edgar, Hume, whose displeasure at the treatment of Edwy and Elgiva is clear enough, remarks, "Such is the ascendant which may be attained, by hypocrisy and cabal, over mankind!" (*History*, I, Chapter II, 122). Hume's judgment is a combination of moral indignation and religious disaffection. In this instance, Hume is pointing up the disproportion between the values of a religious temperament and their secular application.

Like many of his moral judgments, the preceding one evaluated harshly the sacrosanct veil which barbarous activity in the name of religion wrapped around itself. Transactions between church and state were invested with an authority that few would challenge and even fewer question. Religious authority, powerful by itself because of fear and superstition, when joined with secular power could achieve what Hume called an "ascendant" over the

populace. Because of the preeminence of religious customs and
dogmas, any measures taken in behalf of religion were beyond
criticism or correction. In some respects, eighteenth-century England shared this same attitude that anything done in the name of
religion or done to promote piety was sacred and inviolable. That
such an attitude could create much hypocrisy is obvious.

Hume emphasized the barbarity and malfeasance of this kind
of religious hypocrisy in order to show the disruptive influence of
religious authoritarianism when injected into civil and secular
concerns. Despite Locke's eloquent plea in his *Letter concerning
Toleration* (1689), religious power still interposed itself between
the citizen and the state, sometimes with disastrous results, of
which the abortive attempt in 1753 to legalize the naturalization
of Jews is but one example. Whatever its causes and whatever its
effects, Hume deplored the interferences of churchly authority in
civil or secular matters. The *History of England* often relates the
chaos produced by this interference.

Hume is thus sometimes harsh about the foibles and aggran-
dizements of the church or of any institution which attempts tyranny. In contrast to this harshness, the reader finds Hume frequently sympathetic to misfortunes resulting from the frailty of
human nature—if tyranny is absent. An example appears in
Hume's account of King Edgar's quest for suitable bedmates. On
one occasion, Edgar requested at Andover the compliance of his
host's daughter, whose charms had overwhelmed him, for the
night. The mother, determined not to dishonor the family while
nonetheless appearing to acquiesce to the King's impetuosity,
agreed; but she substituted an attractive waiting-maid, Elfleda,
for her daughter. The King, pleased with Elfleda's charms, was
not displeased with the deception and took Elfleda as his favorite
mistress. Shortly after doing so, he heard of the still greater
beauty of a country woman, Elfrida. Wishing to know more, he
sent his favorite, Earl Athelwold, to find out if reports of her
beauty and charm were true. They were, but Athelwold was determined to have her for his own and reported to the King that
her wealth and position had blinded potential suitors to the plain-
ness of her face.

Satisfied with this account, and hearing from Athelwold that he
would like to take Elfrida as his wife in order to improve his own
position, King Edgar relinquished his claim. But clever deceptions

must, unfortunately, come to an end. The King learned of Athelwold's trickery, and demanded to visit him and his new wife. Athelwold cautioned her against revealing the truth for fear of his life, but Elfrida, jealous that she had been deprived of a potential queenship, appeared in all her splendor. Hume concludes his narration in this manner: ". . . she excited at once in his [Edgar's] bosom the highest love towards herself, and the most furious desire of revenge against her husband. He knew, however, to dissemble these passions; and seducing Athelwold into a wood, on pretence of hunting, he stabbed him with his own hand, and soon after publicly espoused Elfrida" (*History,* I, Chapter II, 125). Then Hume simply begins another paragraph by saying "Before we conclude our account. . . ."

To the modern reader, a standard of morality which condemns religious hypocrisy and usurpation of civil power and which seems tacitly to condone the *crime passionel* is at least curious. Yet we cannot shorten Hume's view to fit our own standards. First, he catalogues many more instances of religious chicanery—and judges them harshly—than instances of murder for the sake of sensual gratification. Elsewhere in the *History,* he condemns murders and executions which were thought justifiable to a large number of his countrymen; and his treatment of Charles I is a case in point. We have to remember that he had a most unfavorable opinion of the Dark Ages and Middle Ages, as may be seen in Appendices I and II of the first volume of the *History.* The murder of one person in order to gain his wife seemed, in these times, a common instrument of revenge to Hume. The Anglo-Saxon and Anglo-Norman kings and peoples were barbarians, and he did not expect civilized behavior from them. Finally, we can acknowledge that historians or philosophers have to have more courage to condemn religion than to condemn murder. To disapprove of murder hardly testifies to moral courage, but to disapprove of certain religious activities, in a time when they might be widely condoned or admired, does testify to moral courage. Even so, Hume is almost always harsher upon institutional tyranny than he is on personal, or individual, tyranny.

Tyranny takes many forms, of course, and Hume is particularly sensitive to political tyranny carried out in the homiletics of Christian piety. Although Hume was not an apologist for any form of religion, be it Christian, Jewish, Buddhist, he was inclined to de-

fend minority religions against the impositions of majority ones.
In the reign of Henry III, mentioned in Section I of this chapter,
Hume treats one of the perennial persecutions of the Jews. In it,
we see an example of the way in which the speculative part of his
methodology leads to some of his moral judgments. Disapproving
of the high interest rates in this period (*ca.* 1272), Hume conjectures about the fortunes, literal and figurative, of the Jews: "It is
easy to imagine how precarious their state must have been under
an indigent prince, somewhat restrained in his tyranny over his
native subjects, but who possessed an unlimited authority over the
Jews, the sole proprietors of money in the kingdom, and hated, on
account of their riches, their religion, and their usury: Yet will our
ideas scarcely come up to the extortions which, in fact, we find to
have been practised upon them" (*History,* II, Chapter XII, 225–
26). This conjecture is then supported by a series of instances
demonstrating the ways in which the Jews were tyrannized.

In order to express his distaste for this tyranny, Hume inquires
into the motives of tyrants. They offered as a "better pretence for
extortions, the improbable and absurd accusation, which has been
at different times advanced against that nation . . . that they
crucified a child in derision of the sufferings of Christ. . . . It is
in no wise credible, that even the antipathy born them by the
Christians, and the oppressions under which they laboured, would
ever have pushed them to be guilty of that dangerous enormity"
(*History,* II, Chapter XII, 227). Hume's rhetoric carries with it
tones of disapproval, for he opposed tyranny that hid under the
name of piety. In addition, he suggests that any ensuing violence
would have been the result of the Jews' unstable position. Their
usury, Hume argues, was understandable when recognized as an
attempt to make some compensation for the indignities and the
continual peril that were the whole of their existence.

The acts of violence against the Jews in Henry III's reign Hume
attributes partially to bigotry but primarily to "avidity and rap-
ine." The desire to convert Jews to Christianity by no means cor-
responded to the biblical injunctions to proselytize. For a Jew to
become a Christian and perhaps escape life-long persecution was
a financial hazard: in France, any Jew embracing Christianity for-
feited his real and personal property to the king or any of his
followers. Of this practice, Hume makes the following ironic remark: "These plunderers were careful, lest the profits accruing

from their dominion over that unhappy race should be diminished by their conversion" (*History*, II, Chapter XII, 227). This sentence, incidentally and two others preceding it (which I summarized at the first of this paragraph) did not appear in the first edition, nor in any of the editions published in Hume's lifetime. While I should not argue that this inclusion, made as one of Hume's last revisions, necessarily proves anything, it does indicate Hume's inclination to make moral judgments about popular or unpopular subjects. Along this same line, Hume takes note of the reign of Edward I, successor to Henry III. During Edward's reign a statute was enacted to banish all Jews from England. This banishment Hume attributes to the King's rapacity and zeal and to the poverty of the crown; he describes the King's behavior as "egregious tyranny" (*History*, II, Chapter XIII, 238).

About the time this volume of the *History of England* was being written, the Pelhams were attempting to legalize the naturalization of the Jews, as I noted earlier. Of the Naturalisation Bill, W. E. H. Lecky remarks that "There is no page in the history of the eighteenth century that shows more decisively how low was the intellectual and political condition of English public opinion. According to its opponents, the Jewish Naturalisation Bill sold the birthright of Englishmen for nothing: it was a distinct abandonment of Christianity, it would draw upon England all the curses which Providence had attached to the Jews." [11] Opposition to the bill and prejudice against the Jews was thus widespread and tenacious during the 1750's. For Hume to accuse openly English kings of "egregious tyranny" against the Jews, when many of his countrymen probably would have liked to have had the Jews banished, was not as courageous as his unpopular questionings of religion's postulates. It was, however, a moral judgment that many men, from an excess of prudence, would not have made. Hume sought not special consideration for the Jews by the mere fact of their being Jews, but he objected strongly to their persecution and even more strongly to the trumped-up reasons offered in justification of that persecution.[12]

I have focused briefly on Hume's representation of the treatment of the Jews, although it provides an admittedly artificial method for displaying Hume's penchant for a certain kind of moral judgment in his *History*, a moral judgment which, as we have seen, is often mixed with politics. Clearly, the logic and rhetoric of Hume's various inquiries into the principles of morals in no way fixed the language of his own moral judgments, and he would have been the first, probably, to admit this seeming disparity. His naturalistic ethic left plenty of room for individual moral judgments, which he had no hesitation making. For example, the chicaneries of the Earl of Somerset during the reign of James I earn this reproof: "The favourite had hitherto escaped the inquiry of justice; but he had not escaped that still voice which can make itself be heard amidst all the hurry and flattery of a court, and astonishes the criminal with a just representation of his most secret enormities" (*History,* VI, Chapter XLVII, 75).

Somerset had been charged, along with accomplices and his wife, the countess, with the murder of Sir Thomas Overbury. The accomplices were eventually punished, but Somerset and his wife were pardoned. Of this action, Hume asserts "It must be confessed that James's fortitude had been highly laudable, had he persisted in his first intention of consigning over to severe justice all the criminals: But let us still beware of blaming him too harshly, if on the approach of the fatal hour, he scrupled to deliver into the hands of the executioner, persons whom he had once favoured with his most tender affections" (*History,* VI, Chapter XLVII, 78). A few sentences later, Hume specifically attributes the King's mercy to the "great remains of tenderness which James still felt for Somerset. . . ."

Hume clearly believes that the persistent voice of conscience reminded Somerset of the enormity of his crimes. While we may find no exact corollary in his philosophical writings for this sentiment, we can derive it from Hume's conception of the moral sense. In the *Treatise,* he argued that moral decisions were derived from a moral sense, that morality was something we "felt" rather than judged (*Treatise,* III, i, 2). Hume obviously could not have known whether Somerset had escaped that "still voice," but he assumed a uniformity of sentiment among mankind. Thus, the voice of conscience would be felt as easily in Somerset's time as in Hume's. Although Hume has little sympathy for Somerset, he sympathizes with James's difficulties in punishing a fallen friend. Loyalty Hume recognized as one of the most important virtues, and he frequently admires it in the *History of England,* even when its results are deplorable.

Deplorable results in human transactions were usually mitigated by Hume's sympathetic understanding of human frailty. He made no such concessions to acts born of religious sentiments, but he applauded religious innovations which promoted certain moral principles. The rise of the Independents during the reign of Charles I is a case in point. Here Hume permits an epistemological distinction between two religious sects, the Independents and the Presbyterians, to lead to a qualified approval of the Independents' activities. The "enthusiastic spirit"—or religious fanaticism— of the time encouraged fervent piety: "In proportion to its degree of fanaticism, each sect became dangerous and destructive; and as the independents went a note higher than the presbyterians, they could less be restrained within any bounds of temper and moderation. From this distinction, as from a first principle, were derived, by a necessary consequence, all the other differences of these two sects" (*History*, VII, Chapter LVII, 19).

The Independents opposed the intrusion of clerical authority into secular life, as well as that of the magistrate into religious matters. Believing in none of the hierarchical distinctions of rank set up by other churches, the Independents promulgated the idea that an individual could have instantaneous communication with recognition by God for the purpose of consecration and administration of what few sacraments they accepted. To Hume, all this is very good, and he contrasts their freedom to Catholic dogmatism and to the Presbyterians' elaborate and doctrinaire tenets. As for the Independents, they, "from the extremity of the same zeal, were led into the milder principles of toleration. . . . Of all christian sects this was the first, which, during its prosperity as well as its adversity, always adopted the principle of toleration; and it is remarkable that so reasonable a doctrine owed its origin, not to reasoning, but to the height of extravagance and fanaticism" (*History*, VII, Chapter LVII, 20). Hume's approval is obvious.

The skepticism of Hume's moral principles, I think we have seen, had less influence on his value judgments in the *History of England* than his inclinations and preferences. Frequently he does avoid making a moral or political commitment, either by implication or by direct statement. When the occasion demands that some judgment or evaluation be made, Hume does not shrink from the task. In writing a history of England, he had accepted, as part of his duty, the necessity of pointing out flaws and errors in men and institutions. Although he did not use the *History of Eng-*

land to dramatize his ideas, his philosophical presumptions guided him in the representation of history's events.

I do not wish to suggest that Hume's *History* is totally philosophical. It is "philosophical" only in so far as it reflects his attitudes towards some of the traditional concerns of philosophy; yet almost any history will reflect some of its author's preconceptions about human beings or institutions. Hume's primary occupation in the *History of England* is to dramatize the progress, change, and evolution of constitutional government. While he emphasizes the society and culture of each epoch, his principal interest lies in the improvement of governmental stability, of civil and individual liberty,[13] and of political unity. In his treatment of the data of history, he often reveals the way in which knowledge of the past should illuminate and clarify an age's present problems. In this sense, then, the importance of his *History of England* lies both in its emphasis on constitutional order and its representation of a specific set of moral and political values.

These assertions may not always be applicable to particular events which Hume treats. Any attempt to analyze the *History of England* in terms of a specific concept, prejudice, or faction is automatically doomed to failure. It could be read without reference to any of Hume's other works, but an intensive reading of the *History of England* enlarges our understanding of those other works, and vice versa. Although it has long since been superseded in accuracy by more "scientific" histories of England, it is still one of the most readable histories of England. Few would deny that Hume presented the events, institutions, and characters of English history with clarity, energy, and insight. Even in the 1960's, a newspaper columnist and cracker-barrel philosopher, Harry Golden, mentioned it as one of the seminal works of literature which the student, interested in reading for the sake of reading, ought to read.[14]

CHAPTER 6

Hume and Religious Skepticism

I *Religion and Philosophy:*
"The Natural History of Religion"

THE Reverend William Warburton wrote about Hume's "Natural History of Religion," when it was to be published by Millar:[1] "The design of the first essay is the very same with all Lord Bolingbroke's, to establish *naturalism*, a species of atheism, instead of religion: and he employs one of Bolingbroke's arguments for it. . . . He is establishing atheism; and in one single line of a long essay professes to believe Christianity."[2] Warburton then attributes to Hume a mischief that even the most fanatical anti-Christ could not have accomplished. He was right in perceiving that Hume's piety was outweighed by his skepticism; but, like many otherwise capable minds of the eighteenth century, Warburton was totally incapable of distinguishing between the mildest skepticism and atheism. The only alternative to Christianity or to theism for many eighteenth-century divines was atheism or paganism. Even the Deists, who were aware of greater subtleties in religious inquiries, were often incapable of seeing how different Hume's skepticism was from any brand of atheism.

People like Warburton were doubtlessly irritated not so much by Hume's observations about particular religious problems as they were by his method. "The Natural History of Religion" embodies a historical-anthropological method to account for the "origin of religion in human nature."[3] The statement that religion's origin could be found in human nature and not necessarily in divinity, that it had an origin no more "noble" than any of our passions, surely irritated Warburton and his fellow religionists. Hume has, in other words, not accepted their premises; indeed, he has implicitly argued that the premises for religious argument are faulty. By not accepting the a priori assumptions of traditional theology, Hume confounded his readers and critics; and, by ignor-

125

ing the alleged logic and rightness of their approach, he probably shocked them.

Hume's first argument in "The Natural History of Religion" takes the form of an inquiry into the origins in human nature of belief in a Deity, and he finds that early forms of religion must have been polytheistic. Gradually, as people became more sophisticated, these forms became monotheistic: "The mind rises gradually, from inferior to superior: By abstracting from what is imperfect, it forms an idea of perfection . . ." (*Works*, IV, 311; Root, p. 24). The ideas of perfection thus formed are transferred to some abstract idea of a deity. In early man, Hume argues, the regularity and order of the universe excited no curiosity; and early man assumed that at least one god existed for each phenomenon he did not understand.

In order to emphasize the mystical and quasi-mystical elements in religion, Hume directs attention to our general ignorance about causes, saying that unknown causes create ideas of omnipotence; fear of what we do not know enslaves us. To that which we do not know, we frequently assign a number of human qualities, by finding, for example, human faces in the moon or armies in the clouds. From this propensity, Hume argues, arises a willingness to create a deity for every unexplainable phenomenon. Generally speaking, man tends to allegorize the unknown by means of the known: "And thus, however strong men's propensity to believe invisible, intelligent power in nature, their propensity is equally strong to rest their attention on sensible, visible objects; and in order to reconcile these opposite inclinations, they are led to unite the invisible power with some visible object" (*Works*, IV, 325; Root, p. 38). Hume allows that men are not capable of comprehending an unseen, non-sensible intelligence; and he questions the reasons adduced for assigning as manifestations of that quality certain items or events in the world they do experience.

Two important and interrelated themes emerge from "The Natural History of Religion": (1) Hume regards religious sentiment as one of the passions of mankind; and (2) he finds no logical correlation between the a priori principles of religion and their origin in human nature. Religion thus has no more authority over the human mind, in so far as it is just another passion, than any other passion would have. Because religion deals with supernatural and seemingly unexplainable phenomena, it draws to itself an authority, a certitude missing in other passions; because it offers man exaltation by means of something he cannot comprehend, he assumes that its origin can be only divine.

The logic of the first theme, broken down, leads irrevocably into the second. If man surveys the religious sentiments of any group that have at any time prevailed in the world, he must conclude that they are nothing but "sick men's dreams. . . ." The principles that men attribute to the pervasiveness of a deity in the world are no more to be regarded than the "playsome whimsies of monkies in human shape, than the serious, positive, dogmatical asseverations of a being, who dignifies himself with the name of rational" (*Works*, IV, 362; Root, p. 79).

Hume is asserting that the high-minded, exalting principles that are the theoretics of a religion bear little resemblance to the ways in which they appear in the ordinary world. Men protest mightily of the importance of religion in their lives; yet they act as if they had no confidence in the principles they have embraced. The most intelligent men in all ages have accepted as unquestionable the most absurd and ridiculous theologies, while the most libertine men have advocated some of the most exalted or demanding ideas. The moralities promulgated by many religions have been the most stringent and the most noble in the world, yet they have produced chicanery beyond measure. Finally, Hume continues, death, the surest prospect of mankind, has been assuaged by the promise of the soul's immortality; but not even this security is sufficient to vanquish the terrors of the devout at death's approach.

The questions that Hume has raised in this deceptively short essay are not amenable to easy exegesis, but they are monumentally important to those who find religion either emotionally or intellectually valuable. For a person exhibiting what Hume calls a "delicacy of taste" and who might call it "poignant" or even "poetic," the conclusion is startling: "The whole is a riddle, an ænigma, an inexplicable mystery. Doubt, uncertainty, suspence of judgment appear the only result of our most accurate scrutiny, concerning this subject. But such is the frailty of human reason, and such the irresistible contagion of opinion, that even this deliberate doubt could scarcely be upheld; did we not enlarge our view, and opposing one species of superstition to another, set them a quarrelling; while we ourselves, during their fury and contention, happily make our escape into the calm, though obscure regions of philosophy" (*Works*, IV, 363; Root, p. 76). Those whom William James called the "tough-minded," however, might find the conclusion inescapable.

II *Religion and Philosophy:*
Dialogues concerning Natural Religion

Hume's last work is in many ways his best. Certainly the best-written of his works, it does not suffer from the expansiveness of the *Treatise;* yet the *Dialogues concerning Natural Religion* manages to display almost all of the important philosophical discoveries enunciated in it. Having neither the accessibility nor the range of the two *Enquiries,* it is not, however, the best work for the student just beginning to read Hume; and it is not the one upon which Hume's reputation rests. I think, however, that *Dialogues concerning Natural Religion* is Hume's best work in the sense that it distills all of his thought upon a subject which only the brave dared advocate: religious skepticism. Moreover, it is the most cogent presentation of any religious view in eighteenth-century English literature.

The work consists of a series of intellectual and religious exchanges among three interlocutors: Philo, the skeptic; Cleanthes, the empirical theologian; and Demea, the defender of revealed religion. Their roles are not quantitatively equal because Philo has the greatest percentage of words. Their proportions are, Philo, sixty-seven per cent; Cleanthes, twenty-one per cent; and Demea, twelve per cent.[4] This quantitative disparity carries over into the substance of the arguments. Although Pamphilus, the narrator, whose religious education was charged to Cleanthes, pronounces Cleanthes the victor at the end, this concession is an example of Humean irony.[5] Cleanthes is not merely a straw man, nor is Demea; for they both express certain philosophies of religion affirmed by tradition. If Philo is permitted twice as much to say as the other disputants combined, the imbalance is surely not unjust: for centuries after the birth and death of Christ, the skeptical voice went unheard. Even the emphasis upon *natural* religion, as distinct from supernatural religion, might have made John Knox lament the gross impiety of the age. It is a shocked Demea who protests that both Cleanthes and Philo pay no attention to the a priori arguments not only for God's existence but for his benevolence, omnipotence, and omniscience.

The names that Hume gave to his protagonists are interesting of themselves. Borrowing from Cicero,[6] Hume calls his skeptic Philo; in antiquity, Philo (160–80 B.C.) was the founder of the so-called fourth Academy. Academic philosophy had become synonymous with skeptical philosophy. Cicero studied under Philo; and, in his discourse *De Natura Deorum,* Cotta represents the Academic or skeptical point of view; some of the arguments of Hume's Philo are modeled on Cicero's Cotta. In addition, Cicero's character Balbus is credited with study under the man who succeeded Zeno as head of the Stoic school of philosophy, Cleanthes (331–232 B.C.). Hume's Cleanthes, like Philo, takes some of his arguments and examples from Cicero's Cotta in *De Natura Deorum.*

Other parallels between Cicero and Hume can be found, particularly in the ends of their separate dialogues. Cicero, at the end of *De Natura Deorum,* gives the victory to the orthodox Stoic, Balbus: "Here the conversation ended, and we parted, Velleius thinking Cotta's discourse to be the truer, while I felt that of Balbus approximated more nearly to a semblance of the truth." [7] Pamphilus, the narrator in Hume's *Dialogues,* concludes: "CLEANTHES and PHILO pursued not this conversation much farther; and as nothing ever made greater impression on me, than all the reasonings of that day; so I confess, that, upon a serious review of the whole, I cannot but think, that PHILO's principles are more probable than DEMEA's; but that those of CLEANTHES approach still nearer to the truth" (*Dialogues,* 228).

Authors other than Cicero contribute to the intellectual genealogy of Philo, Cleanthes, and Demea. One of the most likely sources for some of Cleanthes' arguments is Bishop Joseph Butler, author of *The Analogy of Religion* (1736). Butler's *Analogy* and his *Sermons* both employ methods of reasoning markedly similar to the expositions of Cleanthes.[8] While Butler supplies some of the method for Cleanthes, other authors supply, in some instances, exact words; for Hume relied upon the scientific theism of two of Newton's disciples, Dr. George Cheyne and Colin Macluarin, whose arguments he has employed almost word for word in some places.[9] Preserved Smith suggests that Cleanthes represents

John Locke; his key to the identity of the characters in the *Dialogues* is at least curious: "Cleanthes, derived from the Greek words for 'lock' and 'flower,' is John Locke, the flower of philosophy and the champion of the intellectual argument for the reasonableness of Christianity." [10] Still another commentator, who has identified Cleanthes as a "follower of Locke," observes that he is actually "Hume's portrait of Bishop [George] Berkeley." [11] Cleanthes' thought, however meager it may be in proportion to Philo's, is certainly respectable; and the various viewpoints he reflects certainly imply that he is not a philosophical pantywaist. In fact, a number of commentators have thought Cleanthes to be Hume. [12]

Demea is even more of a problem than Cleanthes. His religious principles are totally a priori, and he thinks that religion cannot be validated by empirical arguments, not because of religion's weakness but because its evidence is not conformable to human experience. Joseph Milner, whose reaction to the publication of the *Dialogues* was examined in Chapter 1, said of Demea, "I have taken no notice of Hume's Demea, because I cannot find a feature of Christianity about him. Dr. [Samuel] Clark's metaphysicks and the Gospel, have, I think, no sort of connection." [13] The connection, which Milner disputes, between Demea and Dr. Samuel Clarke, the well-known intellectualist and rationalistic theologian, is tenuous; but it is nevertheless there. [14]

Hume found Clarke's metaphysical pronouncements just a little bit silly, and Demea appears just that, in all of his shock and bewilderment at Philo's and Cleanthes' failure to use a priori arguments to prove the existence of God. For a reader to see Demea as Clarke implies some intellectual capability on Demea's part; yet Demea's view has been said to represent that of the common people: "Demea, from the Greek word meaning 'common people,' presents the ordinary opinions of the masses." [15] From the mathematical principles which Clarke had attempted to use as a model for his religious rationalism, to the skeptical principles of Pierre Bayle or to the mystical ones of Father Nicolas Malebranche is a long step; but it has been taken: " 'Demea' speaks in the manner of the French thinkers, Pierre Bayle, the skeptic, and the mystical Malebranche." [16] While no one has so far identified Hume as Demea, I should think the range of differences about Demea's intellectual heritage would suggest that Hume, while treating Demea ironically, did not make him an ignoramus.

The identification of Philo as Hume is easy to make. Philo's skeptical principles, his method of argument, his indifference to threats of eternal damnation, and his unwillingness to acquiesce to the gospels as the final authority in matters of fact exactly resemble the philosophical positions of David Hume. Preserved Smith has identified Philo as Hume by pointing out that "Philo means 'beloved,' just as 'David' does, and hence may be identified with Hume himself." [17] Hume's first biographer, John Hill Burton, states that Philo appears "first as a materialist of the Spinoza school . . ." and then as a "sceptical demolisher . . ."; and he also identifies Cleanthes as Hume. [18] Professor Hendel avers that "'Philo' seems to be a Francis Bacon, empirically-minded in science but skeptical toward reasoned knowledge in religion." [19]

Despite these identifications, and none of them is unreasonable, contemporary opinion, like some of that in Hume's own time, has generally concluded that Philo is Hume and that Hume would not be comfortable as Cleanthes. [20] Some exceptions have been those who have thought that Hume was, in truth, the narrator, Pamphilus. [21] As we have seen, Hume chose the names of his interlocutors carefully, with a view to their Classical fittingness. In *De Natura Deorum*, Cotta, the skeptic, speaks of a Pamphilus who was a student of Plato and says that Pamphilus was ridiculed by Epicurus. That Hume, whose philosophy was about as anti-Platonic as possible for the eighteenth century, would permit a Platonist, a man whose philosophy he scorned, to pass judgment on the arguments in the *Dialogues* is most unlikely.

I have gone into the intellectual homologues of Hume's characters in some detail because I think we ought to be aware of both the learning and the precision that went into the composition of the *Dialogues*. The various identifications of the interlocutors implies that a considerable amount of knowledge, if not tradition, went into their composition. One reason this work engages our attention repeatedly lies in its richness, a richness which is the result of years of speculative thought and knowledge.

The chief concern of the *Dialogues* is an extended analysis of both the phenomenological evidence for the existence and benevolence of God and the proper way in which that evidence can be used. The method of this analysis finds Cleanthes employing the argument from design to establish the existence of a perfect, immutable, and divinely created order in the universe, while Philo raises objections to the logic Cleanthes employs. (Demea's arguments are all a priori and rationalistic.) Hume had taken notice of the design argument in the *Treatise* and there he seemed to accept its validity:

> The same imperfection [lack of an impression in the external world] attends our ideas of the Deity; but this can have no effect either on religion or morals. The order of the universe proves an omnipotent mind; that is, a mind whose will is constantly attended with the obedience of every creature and being. Nothing is more requisite to give a foundation to all the articles of religion, nor is it necessary we shou'd form a distinct idea of the force and energy of the supreme Being.[22]

Hume's statement differs from others in a century in which obedience to the will of God and the insignificance of man in comparison to God were parts of the rhetorical style of philosophical writings. Hume means by an omnipotent mind one whose will is constantly obeyed—a definition that conforms to natural laws. To disobey the laws of the universe is patently impossible for man, but he can disobey such things as gospel exhortations; that is, he can ignore the biblical injunction "Thou shalt not kill," but he can hardly ignore the law of gravity. Still, Hume suggests that our knowledge of natural law is sufficient to underwrite the laws of religion.

One such admission, however, does not a theology make. Hume's other pronouncements in his *Essays* and *Enquiries* all examine the phenomenological evidence adduced in support of some theological principle and find it wanting. Moreover, Demea as a character illustrates the unpopularity of the design argument with proponents of supernatural, revealed religion. Frequently associated with Deism, the design argument was thought to rob religion of its autonomy and authority, if not of its mystery and beauty. After all, if the ways of God were revealed in man's subjective experience of everyday events, how could the experience of life after death be as exciting as the gospels promised?

Part I of the *Dialogues* opens with a few pious observations

about the desirability of impressing early upon children the principles of religion, but almost immediately Philo tries to gain assent
about the "narrow limits of human reason" in matters of religion.
Cleanthes accuses Philo of skepticism, but he accuses him of Pyrrhonism rather than the peculiarly Humean brand of skepticism.
In fact, Cleanthes iterates some of the psychological limitations of
skepticism in very much the same manner Hume had done in the
Treatise.[23] Philo's skepticism concerns itself both with the ade-
quacy and the nature of the evidence adduced in support of propositions about the conceptions we have of God. He asks about the
justification, if any, for the selection of whatever criteria would
make up a theological discussion. Concerned not so much with
the traditional question "Does God exist?"—or with any other
question that does not lend itself to positive, empirical answers—
Philo interrogates Demea and Cleanthes about the methodology
to be used in an inquiry into natural religion. The promises of and
possibilities in natural religion are not, he points out, of the same
kind as those related to commerce or politics; before we can
"anatomize" natural religion, we must at the very least wonder
about our intellectual suitability for such a task.

At the conclusion of Part I, Philo implicitly questions the ways
in which evidence of any kind has been used in the history of
religious thought. Remarking on the "strong symptoms of priest-
craft" in the progress of religious thought, Philo observes that un-
orthodox religious sentiments arose from "presumptuous questions
of received opinions" and from a belief that human reason could
solve all problems. In the present age (the eighteenth century),
however, scholars and divines speak of the reasonableness of
Christianity since it suits their purposes better than an appeal to
mystery. Religious men have, in other words, sought by any
means what they thought was a desirable end: "Thus, sceptics in
one age, dogmatists in another; whichever system best suits the
purpose of these reverend gentlemen, in giving them an ascendant over mankind, they are sure to make it their favourite principle, and established tenet" (*Dialogues*, 139–40).

To this statement, Cleanthes retorts that men ought to embrace
principles which confute the "cavils of atheists, libertines, and
freethinkers of all denominations" because such a confutation
would be a strong presumption of the truth of the principles. This
concession is strategically important for Philo, for he has gotten

Cleanthes to confess that he is really less interested in pursuing truth than in upholding religious doctrine. Yet Philo never reminds Cleanthes of this statement, and its implications escape the notice of both Cleanthes and Demea. As the discussion progresses and as the argument from design is turned back again and again, Hume's strategy is clear: Cleanthes' principles are more elocutionary than philosophical, more expedient than cogent.

This judgment may seem harsh in view of Cleanthes' abilities, but he is in fact more interested in the empirical establishment of religion than in the means by which that establishment is achieved. True, he does not confine his theology to a posteriori arguments, does not condone the hypotheses of Demea; and his basic maneuver, the design argument, is never forsaken. Yet he is unwilling within this area to accept any of Philo's criticism. His basic argument is articulated fully in Part II:

Look round the world: Contemplate the whole and every part of it: You will find it to be nothing but one great machine, subdivided into an infinite number of lesser machines, which again admit of subdivisions, to a degree beyond what human senses and faculties can trace and explain. All these various machines, and even their most minute parts, are adjusted to each other with an accuracy, which ravishes into admiration all men, who have ever contemplated them. The curious adapting of means to ends, throughout all nature, resembles exactly, though it much exceeds, the productions of human contrivance; of human design, thought, wisdom, and intelligence. Since therefore the effects resemble each other, we are led to infer, by all the rules of analogy, that the causes also resemble; and that the Author of nature is somewhat similar to the mind of man; though possessed of much larger faculties, proportioned to the grandeur of the work, which he has executed. By this argument *a posteriori,* and by this argument alone, we do prove at once the existence of a Deity, and his similarity to human mind and intelligence. (*Dialogues,* 143)[24]

Hume's ironic strategy in the *Dialogues* leads him to select Demea, not Philo, to reply to Cleanthes' argument. Demea, astonished at Cleanthes' failure to employ a priori proofs and abstract arguments, he approves of neither Cleanthes' conclusion nor his manner of reaching it.

Philo responds to Cleanthes by appearing to agree with Demea about the faults in Cleanthes' *method,* but he actually disagrees with Cleanthes' *reasonings*. Philo points out that, when a previously occurred event presents itself again, we draw without hesitation the accustomed inference as, for example, that a rock in the air will fall if unsupported. Strong similarity in a particular series of events assures us of recurrence. Departure from the similarity decreases the probability, and the evidence may so decrease as to produce a very weak analogy; and this imperfect analogy is often confuted by additional experience. Continuing his argument, Philo states that the sight of a house leads us to infer a builder, but Cleanthes could surely not affirm that the universe has such a resemblance to a house, that such a resemblance would lead us to infer a similar cause with the same certainty as we would in the case of the house. Nor would we have so perfect an analogy.

To strengthen his argument, Philo comes to a more damaging objection, that a man is not able, without the aid of experience, to determine what is and what is not fact, or what is the actual state of the universe. Being unable to call anything impossible which he can conceive, he must give every "chimera of his fancy" an equal footing; for each would be equally plausible in the absence of experience. The mind will not and cannot supply a cause without experience; one must allow that "order, arrangement, or the adjustment of final causes is not, of itself, any proof of design . . ." (*Dialogues*, 146). Matter does not organize itself into something regular and ordered, but the mind organizes matter and material into various coherent units.

Restating his arguments in a more powerful form, Philo points out that Cleanthes is assuming that the universe falls into the same category of causality as houses, ships, and machines, and that the causal connection implying design is different only in degree, not in kind. We cannot, according to Philo, legitimately assume that thought, design, and intelligence are the activating springs and principles of the universe any more than we can say that heat and cold are; nor can we logically assume that what we find causally operative in the world of our experience will be so for the universe as a whole. Our limited experience of what we call "cause and effect" does not establish the origin and existence of nature as a whole; the operations of a part of nature do not allow us to reach any just conclusions about the totality of nature.

Philo then asks Cleanthes if he is not mistaken in assuming that intelligence, and it alone, could be the organizing and designing principle of the universe. Nature, having in her possession numerous manners of operation, would not necessarily rely just on thought or intelligence for her creations. Now Philo bolsters his assertion that the causal connections implying design are different in kind, not just in degree as Cleanthes supposed: "When two *species* of objects have always been observed to be conjoined together, I can *infer*, by custom, the existence of one wherever I *see* the existence of the other: And this I call an argument from experience" (*Dialogues,* 149). Since we have no experience of the origin of a universe, we have no compelling reason to infer a causal connection between the elements of our experience and the creation of a universe by an omnipotent mind.

To Cleanthes' objection that it is not necessary to have observed the origin of a universe or to be in a position to see the earth move to know that it moves, Philo replies that the movement of other planets and celestial bodies, by virtue of their analogy and resemblance to ours, confirms the Copernican hypothesis. No ground for a distinction between terrestrial and celestial things exists, and the analogy is valid in comparing the two. But the argument from design can appeal to no analogies so valid and consistent as these. The argument from design nowhere offers analogies nearly so certain as those of the Copernican system.

The arguments just outlined, which appear in Part II of the *Dialogues,* constitute, with a few exceptions, the crux of the arguments Hume brings against the argument from design. They are, in a manner of speaking, a "theme and variations"; for the same attack appears throughout the *Dialogues* but with significant and informative variations each time. Even the several manners of statement are themselves merely elaborate variations and explanations of Hume's skepticism about the necessity of causal inference between two contiguous events. In essence, Hume asks if there is anything in the universe that logically, necessarily, and inexorably implies its creation by an omnipotent mind. If so, does anything in the nature and arrangement of the universe imply that its creation stems from a benevolent and altruistic Deity, who also thoughtfully arranged that such a universe would have a strict and inescapable eschatology? Although Philo's questions are not rhetorical, he suggests that neither he nor Cleanthes can answer them.

Hereafter, Cleanthes would seem to be on the defensive, although he has taken a lesson from either politics or football and has made his defense a good offense. He is on the defensive only in the sense that he ignores or fails to understand Philo's objections. Part III opens with Cleanthes' reply to Philo that his arguments are "absurd," and "no better than abstruse cavils. . . ." He asserts, in a rhetorical question, that "the similarity of the works of nature to those of art . . . is self-evident and undeniable" (*Dialogues*, 152). To refute Philo's contentiousness requires no more than an enunciation of illustrations and examples of his (Cleanthes') basic principles because the similarities between any two separate kinds of creation are so great as to overwhelm logic.

Cleanthes employs two examples to refute Philo, again taking advantage of the rhetorical question to imply that Philo is more stubborn than perspicacious. He first asks Philo what his conclusion would be should he hear a voice in the sky, speaking more loudly than any human voice, and instructing mankind, in the language of each nation, in some sentiment appropriate to a benevolent Deity. Philo could conclude only that the cause of this voice entailed some purpose or design. Of course, Cleanthes agrees, such a thing has never happened; but it is the kind of reasonable analogy that supports the idea of design. The analogy Cleanthes suggests is this: when we hear an articulate voice and do not see the speaker, we assume that the person speaking exists. The voice from the skies, however, is unlike any human voice; but the only experience we have of voices is that they issue from intelligent causes. Therefore, we assume that this voice must issue from an intelligence far greater than ours. Cleanthes' second example to refute Philo draws attention to a library containing volumes of "the most refined reason and exquisite beauty" (*Dialogues*, 153). The original causes of these volumes, he argues, must have been intelligence, because we have no experience of books like these arising any other way.

The point of Cleanthes' two examples is that human experience can be projected beyond the mundane to the divine. In essence, Cleanthes' logic here is relational, that is, he is saying X is to Y as X_1 is to Y_1. Substituting Cleanthes' propositions for that logical shorthand, we have the following: our knowledge of mundane events bears the same relation to their cause in the same manner that our knowledge of divine events bears a relation to their cause. Philo attacks this logic by saying that Cleanthes is equating experience with knowledge. Although they have both agreed that knowledge must come from experience and from reasoning in the light of experience, Philo had pointed out in Part II that we have had no experience of divine events: "Our ideas reach no farther than our experience: We have no experience of divine attributes and operations: I need not conclude my syllogism: You can draw the inference for yourself" (*Dialogues*, 142–43). Thus, Philo will accept neither a syllogistic nor a relational logic for a proof of God's existence. Cleanthes is asserting a relation between mundane causes and divine causes that is based not upon experience but upon intuition. Philo's syllogism is intended to clarify the intuitional character of Cleanthes' logic.

Yet it is not Philo who replies to the arguments of Cleanthes; Hume even has Pamphilus say of Philo that he was "a little embarrassed and confounded . . ." (*Dialogues*, 155). Demea replies to Cleanthes' assertions and argues that Cleanthes' proofs of God's existence have a great force because of their familiarity. Insisting that the ways of God are not those of man, Demea develops the earlier implications of his theory of the incomprehensibility of God's attributes; what we experience in nature, he says, is but a small part of God's totality which must remain unknown to our earthly existence. To draw analogies between the mind of God and that of man makes us guilty, according to Demea, of "the grossest and most narrow partiality . . ." (*Dialogues*, 156).

Hume's strategy here is to let the conservative theologian, exemplified by Demea, make a more severe criticism than Philo could have without being charged with impiety or infidelity. In a paragraph added to Part III when he was revising it, probably in 1775, Hume has Demea elaborate upon Philo's syllogism of Part II. Since our ideas are derived from our senses, Demea says, they must be false and illusionary and cannot therefore originate in divine intelligence. We have no idea of what constitutes divine intelligence, and we can in no way compare the human way of thinking to the divine way. The language we use to define human thought cannot be used as a meta-language for divine thought. Demea's a priori conclusion is one to which Hume could give at least partial assent: "the infirmities of our nature do not permit us to reach any ideas, which in the least correspond to the ineffable sublimity of the divine attributes" (*Dialogues*, 157).

Cleanthes' reply opens Part IV of the *Dialogues*. Cleanthes is astonished that Demea should join the skeptics and atheists who insist upon the unknowability of God or of the first cause. Demea rightly accuses him of name-calling and implies that he himself could respond in kind by assigning the term "anthropomorphite" to Cleanthes. Stating Hume's concept of the self, Demea asserts both the qualitative and the quantitative differences between the selfhood of men and that of God. Cleanthes is not, however, overwhelmed; and he makes a lucid and philosophically important reply: "A mind, whose acts and sentiments and ideas are not distinct and successive; one, that is wholly simple, and totally immutable; is a mind which has no thought, no reason, no will, no sentiment, no love, no hatred; or in a word, is no mind at all. It is an abuse of terms to give it that appellation; and we may as well speak of limited extension without figure, or of number without composition" (*Dialogues*, 159).

Cleanthes has used Demea's previous linguistic criticism against him. If we have no words within our language with which God can be appropriately described, then we are hard-pressed to assert any proposition, a priori or a posteriori, about Him. Our mind must bear something more than a perfunctory resemblance to God's mind unless we insist that God's mind is literally unknowable. And if His mind is literally unknowable because it is totally different from ours, we would have no criteria for recognizing knowledge of God when it was thrust upon us. Not even divine revelation could have any force because it would be expressed in a manner whose accuracy we could never possibly verify—emotionally, physically, or intellectually. To know God, or even God's attributes, we must have a means of knowing; and Demea's principles are self-vitiating.

Philo does not reply directly to Cleanthes; he simply reinforces his earlier criticisms of the design argument. He points out that the assignation of one particular cause to one event does not explain the cause of that cause. In extrapolating from our experience certain human events that "prove" design in the world and hence an "Author of nature," we lead ourselves into a series of infinitely regressing causes. Whatever procedure or methodology we may use to prove design in nature, we can never escape human curiosity; when we go one step beyond our experience in the search for causes, we cannot help inviting an infinite regression. Philo even suggests a method which Cleanthes could pursue but wisely does not: "By supposing [the present material world] to contain the principle of its order within itself, we really assert it to be God; and the sooner we arrive at that Divine Being so much the better" (*Dialogues*, 162).

Cleanthes replies to this criticism by saying that once he has found his Deity, he is content to go no farther. And in Part V, after Philo has reasserted the unique quality of the creation of the world, a quality of which we have no experience, Cleanthes affirms that the hypothesis of design recurs in all of Philo's arguments; this concession he regards as a "sufficient foundation for religion." This discussion advances iconoclastically enough through Part VI, and in Part VII some of the drama begins to unfold when Philo points out that the universe bears a greater resemblance to animal bodies and vegetables than to the productions of human art.

If Cleanthes agrees with his previous contention that like causes produce like results, then he must agree that the origin of the world should be attributed to generation or vegetation rather than to reason or design. A comet's tail, Philo says, can contain the "seed" of a new world; and the metaphor of vegetation would seem to be more informing and accurate than the hypothesis of design. Oddly enough, it is Demea who makes a strongly Humean criticism of this reasoning: "What *data* have you for such extraordinary conclusions? And is the slight, imaginary resemblance of the world to a vegetable or an animal sufficient to establish the same inference with regard to both?" (*Dialogues*, 177).

And Philo agrees with him. He was, he says, simply demonstrating a way in which Cleanthes' logic, pushed to its inescapable implications, defeats his own arguments. After some second thoughts, Demea opines that the vegetative quality of the world, if true, would be still another instance of the validity of the argument from design. From what other faculty but design could such an organizing principle spring? Philo could reply to this argument by re-establishing the argument against infinitely regressing causes; instead, he indicates that Demea is begging the question, that he has assumed thought to be the *only* source of order. In his most famous example of an hypothesis as valid as Cleanthes' design hypothesis, Philo postulates a world inhabited by spiders. The Brahmins had asserted that the world was spun from the belly of an infinite spider. Although this sort of cosmogony appears ridiculous to human beings, it would not in a world inhabited by spiders. A spider obviously spins out an orderly web, and little imagination is required to see that order could come from the belly as well as the brain. Cleanthes, astonished by the fertility of Philo's invention, states that he does not know how to answer all these examples; and he asserts that these whimsical conjectures may puzzle, but they will never convince us.

Philo's inventiveness has indeed overwhelmed Cleanthes, although Philo ascribes his creativity to the suppositions contained in the study of natural religion. Taking a different tack, Cleanthes questions Philo about the adaptability of man to the earth and suggests that the numerous instances of conveniences afforded man by the world are instances of design—and of a benevolent one at that. To this inquiry, Philo replies that in all our experience our "ideas are copied from real objects . . ." (*Dialogues*, 186). Cleanthes reverses this order and gives thought precedence in the formation of matter; yet we have never experienced such an order. Thought cannot order matter, at least so far as we know; and the hypothesis of design runs up against that insuperable barrier.

To conclude his remarks and to end this section of the *Dialogues*, Philo remarks upon the difficulties attendant upon all religious systems, and the passage is reminiscent of the conclusion found in "The Natural History of Religion." While the theologians quarrel with each other, they perform a service whose value they would surely question: "But all of them, on the whole, prepare a complete triumph for the *sceptic;* who tells them, that no system ought ever to be embraced with regard to such subjects: For this plain reason, that no absurdity ought ever to be assented to with regard to any subject. A total suspense of judgment is here our only *reasonable* resource" (*Dialogues*, 186–87 [my italics]).

At the opening of Part IX, Demea agrees with Philo about the difficulties attending a posteriori arguments and says for that reason we ought to accept without question the sublimity of the a priori argument. Nothing can exist without a cause, Demea asserts; to avoid an infinitely regressing series of causes, we must finally fall back upon some "ultimate cause that is necessarily existent . . ." (*Dialogues*, 188). Without a necessarily existent being, we could attribute probability to any supposition or to the existence of nothing since eternity. We cannot accept a necessarily existent Being who is His own reason for existence, and whose non-existence cannot be imagined without involving ourselves in a contradiction.

Before Philo has a chance to demolish this particular piece of metaphysics, Cleanthes does it for him by pointing out, among other things, that the words "necessary existence" have no ascertainable meaning. Hume's permitting Cleanthes to answer Demea is another instance of his strategic irony. He is now in a position to subvert not only the argument from design, which he has in fact already done, but also to render inefficacious all the ontological or otherwise non-empirical arguments for God's existence. The drama of the *Dialogues*, begun in Part VII, is now approaching its climax.

Part IX of the *Dialogues* concludes with Philo's first manifestation of skepticism about the conviction the a priori argument is supposed to bring. Demea, who makes no reply in the opening paragraph of Part X to this observation of Philo's, merely asseverates that each man feels within him the vital truth of religion. And Philo concurs, for the time being, in Demea's contention that religion is responsible for whatever morality man may have. The interlocutors raise some familiar problems—evil, man's inhumanity to man, the innate goodness or wickedness of man—but little is said to advance a proof of God's existence. Observing that man can surmount animals and all his real enemies, Philo adds that he cannot disencumber himself of his imaginary enemies, those that haunt his imagination and terrify him, yet have no real existence.

Cleanthes, who finds Philo's observations revealing, agrees that, if he can prove mankind to be innately corrupt and miserable, then religion can have no real value. Religion can little profit by the establishing of the natural attributes of the Deity when his moral attributes can be doubted. To this Demea replies, not yet seeing the vast disagreement between himself and Philo, that the life on earth is but a moment in comparison to eternity and implies that all the events of nature work toward universal good. Finding Demea guilty of hypothesis-building, Cleanthes strongly advocates that the only way one can verify divine benevolence is by denying the "misery and wickedness of man." Philo, too much of an empiricist for this assertion, challenges Cleanthes to prove the non-existence of misery by reflecting upon the various qualities of pain mankind endures. Philo can agree with Cleanthes that the order of the universe strikes us on occasion with enough force to support the design argument. To view mankind from any direction, however, can in no wise support a view of universal morality, unless we do the greatest violence to logic; only the "eyes of faith" can perceive the moral attributes of the world.

The discussion of evil is amplified in Part XI with some impressive insights.[25] Philo's rhetoric points up the irony of pretending to ourselves that the blind workings of nature can be called "good," when we are surrounded by so much "evil." His long exposition, however, finally reveals to Demea the vast distance between their views when compared to the paradoxical closeness of their initial procedure. When Philo asserts that evil in the world must have a cause but does not accept Demea's a priori notions of future rewards, Demea is astonished: "Hold! Hold! cried DEMEA: Whither does your imagination hurry you? I joined in alliance with you, in order to prove the incomprehensible nature of the divine Being, and refute the principles of CLEANTHES, who would measure every thing by a human rule and standard. But I now find you running into all the topics of the greatest libertines and infidels; and betraying that holy cause, which you seemingly espoused. Are you secretly, then, a more dangerous enemy than CLEANTHES himself?" Cleanthes answers for him: "And are you so late in perceiving . . . ? Philo, from the beginning, has been amusing himself at both our expense; and it must be confessed, that the injudicious reasoning of our vulgar theology has given him but too just a handle of ridicule" (*Dialogues*, 212–13).

The high point of the drama in the *Dialogues* is now reached. Demea is not merely content with the recognition of Philo's purpose; he finds some pretense to leave the company of Cleanthes and Philo. Had he remained, he might have more fully appreciated Hume's strategy. Few will doubt that Philo and Demea could agree on the single most important postulate in any discourse about God's existence: that a posteriori proofs can never be convincing because of the failures in logic, and the surest approach to knowledge of God must be an act of faith. To affirm that "God exists" is not an empirical proposition but an act of faith. There, however, the agreement would end; for Demea would want to introduce a priori and abstract arguments for

God's existence; and, as Philo earlier implies, these would have cogency only for those who are already convinced or who never really doubted.

Demea's petulant departure thus dramatizes the failure of the a priori theologians to see that they had something in common with the skeptic. Unfortunately, they were too busy calling skeptics "libertines and infidels" to see the ironic correctness of Philo's last utterance in the *Dialogues:* "To be a philosophical sceptic is, in a man of letters, the first and most essential step towards being a sound, believing Christian . . ." (*Dialogues* 228). The second step, the act of faith, is not so essential, but is much harder to make, because it is individual, unique, and empirically incomprehensible. We need hardly add that Philo never made the second step. He agrees *"that the cause or causes of order in the universe probably bear some remote analogy to human intelligence,"* but he thinks the ways of God to man would be more amply and aptly illustrated "by affording some more particular revelation to mankind, and making discoveries of the nature, attributes, and operations of the divine object of our Faith" (*Dialogues,* 227). Philosophy is likely to prove small aid to the "haughty dogmatist" who would erect a system of belief upon the inadequate evidence of our senses; a man sensitive to the "revealed truth" of religion will more readily accept faith, not empiricism and reason, as his guide to religious insight.

So ends Hume's cogent, yet deliberately inconclusive, inquiry into natural religion. The major achievement was to lay to rest any pretense to validity that the argument from design might have had. Accepting Hume's reasonings and his conclusions, the reader can, as Hume did, prefer to go no farther than that first step into skepticism. The leap from skepticism to an act of faith crosses a gulf whose depth and width cannot be measured in any language known to man.

CHAPTER 7

David Hume: Man of Letters

SINCE Hume wrote neither fiction nor poetry, he is not usually regarded as a "literary" figure, at least in the twentieth century. Readers in the eighteenth century thought of him both as a "philosopher" (in the much broader eighteenth-century sense of that term) and as a controversial essayist; nineteenth-century readers regarded him primarily as a historian, and his *History of England* went through approximately ninety editions in the nineteenth century; young twentieth-century readers think of Hume as a philosopher and are frequently surprised to learn that he wrote a history of England. That the twentieth century has chosen, for whatever reasons, to exclude philosophical lucidity and historical perspective as two of the defining qualities of literature is perhaps lamentable, but understandable in terms of the rage for ready-made classifications of any material requiring intellectual evaluation.

This twentieth-century attitude towards Hume is not easily documented, although his omission from college and university classes in English literature and English history could serve as a starting-point. More tangible evidence can be found in reviews of books about Hume. When Professor Mossner produced *The Forgotten Hume* in 1943, he observed, perhaps a bit extravagantly, that "In sober truth, it must be put on the record that, with a single important exception, [Dr. Samuel] Johnson's imposing literary production did not equal Hume's, whether in quality, in scope, or in influence. The exception was the *Dictionary*" (p. 195). To almost any eighteenth-century scholar or critic of today, that statement was an immediate challenge. In reviewing the book, Professor René Wellek took Professor Mossner to task for his assertion by asking in what way Johnson's work was inferior to Hume's and by replying: "Surely not in literary quality, in imagination, in style, in critical ideas on literature, in sheer personality

145

and character. All these are qualities which count for more in *literature* than Hume's philosophical mind, his power of analysis, and even his lucidity of style and skill of exposition." [1] Thus, one of the most important twentieth-century critics places Hume's achievement in the "realm of thought"—and apparently not in *"literature."*

Time has at least vindicated Hume of one of Professor Wellek's observations in the same review that "The man Hume will remain, except for biographers, the 'forgotten Hume,' however good he might have been." Instead, Hume does elicit a sympathetic response from many modern readers who appreciate his wit, his irony, his urbanity. As a result, he is no longer "forgotten"; he is being read as much and perhaps more than he was in the eighteenth century, to judge from the number of recent reprints of his various works. What, then, we may ask, are the reasons for reading Hume today?

First of all, I think we read Hume in order to learn something about men's ways of thinking about their environments, their customs, their attitudes, and their limitations. Hume applied his considerable powers of analysis to almost every subject concerned with the life of the mind. His writings are valuable because of his attempts to explain, for example, why tragedy in drama affects us as it does and why it creates pleasurable sensations in us when the "real thing" would disgust or frighten us. His own reasons for writing are, in fact, similar to our reasons for reading him. Unlike some other authors of the eighteenth century, Hume's reasons for writing were not totally mercenary. Applying his energies to intellectual problems, he found, in their complexities, enough material for a lifetime of reflection and exposition.

Hume's primary interest was not peculiar to his age: he sought to expand where practical the boundaries of knowledge. However, Hume also sought to fence off those areas (like school metaphysics) that pretended to knowledge but were empty. For every intellectual discipline which engaged his interest, he tried to formulate the principles appropriate to its study. In many instances, he discarded old methods of inquiry because of their inherent limitations. The new method he proposed was, in almost every instance, guided either by his skepticism or by what he called the "experimental method of reasoning." Where others began inquiries into the "laws of nature" in terms of cause and effect, he questioned the validity of causal imputations. Where others began inquiries into religious matters by assuming the existence of a benevolent Deity, he questioned the evidence for that assumption. We read Hume, then, for exactly those qualities that Professor Wellek described—for style, for literary quality, and for imaginative observations about human nature. While Hume's style is by no means perfect, it is eminently readable; and it contains a number of fine pieces of rhetoric that have the same immediate appeal as some of Dr. Johnson's aphorisms and witticisms. In fact, the similarities and differences in the two men's styles are instructive. Both men's styles are marked by a reliance upon the vocabulary of science; Hume makes metaphorical us of a number of Newtonian concepts, while Johnson's style is partially derived from writers like Dr. George Cheyne, Dr. John Arbuthnot, and Sir Thomas Browne.[2] Dr. Johnson's prose style is sometimes ironic, often moralistic, almost always didactic. Hume's style is less frequently didactic, less openly moralistic, and more subtly ironic. Johnson's vocabulary is more extensive than Hume's, and more ornate; but Hume is given to sentences more complicated than Johnson's. Both men exhibited the tendency of their age for the long, involved sentence.

Hume's imaginative use of language can be found in the analogies and metaphors with which he described and defined certain human activities and other phenomena; we saw some examples in Chapter 2. More interested in accurate representation or analysis than in the glib phrase, he could nevertheless compound some rhetorically fascinating phrases, of which "Reason is, and ought only to be, etc.," "Whatever *is*, may *not* be," and the conclusion of the first *Enquiry* are good examples. More importantly, his imagination suggested logical alternatives or antitheses in discourses where they had been neither conceived nor conjectured. When analogies were offered in support of natural phenomena, Hume offered another analogy, one just as plausible, which demonstrated the infinite variety of causes which could be invoked to account for any given event. His imagination expressed itself in expository constructs, not in fictionalized or "creative" representations of life or "Nature."

The best sustained examples of Hume's literary skills are the *History*, the *Enquiry concerning Human Understanding*, and the *Dialogues*. In the *History*, Hume handles a vast amount of information in an easy manner; indeed, his narrative is a decided improvement over the accumulated verbiage of his predecessors. In the *Dialogues,* a work Hume polished for several years, he handles a number of intricate ideas with grace and energy. We do not say that the *Dialogues* is easy reading: we are even likely to miss the subtleties of Hume's thought because of the attractive prose. But these works, like all of his writings (with the exception of the essays he termed "frivolous"), exhibit Hume's enduring qualities: they all have ideas as their logical core. For Hume, meaning is the most important component of any writing. Even in the essays that he withdrew from circulation he invariably attempted some meaningful inquiry in each, however light or easy the tone may have been. He was neither adept at writing frothy and clever essays whose only value lay in momentary diversion, nor did he cultivate seriousness for its own sake. He recognized the values of irony and raillery, and they were constant companions to his ideas.

Hume's literary achievements are found in the quality of his prose, in the imaginative projections of his skepticism, and in the lucidity of his exposition. Having attempted (so far as we know) neither fiction nor poetry,[3] he cannot be labeled an outstanding "literary" figure in the strictest sense of that word. Yet he brought to philosophy, history, and politics many literary qualities with the result that all were mutually improved. He thought of himself as a "man of letters," which is indeed the best way of describing him. Alexander Pope had observed in a famous couplet in his *Essay on Criticism* that *"True Wit* is *Nature* to Advantage drest,/ What oft was *Thought,* but ne'er so well Exprest" (297–98). Hume was thinking what was *not* often thought, and he could not seek new ways of expressing old insights.

Although he falls short of this criterion of Pope's, he easily meets another: that of having ideas as the controlling unity in one's writing. In evaluating Hume's literary significance, then, we cannot call him a stylistic innovator or developer, but we cannot separate ideas from literature. To do that would be to advocate a literature that appeals solely to the senses, where no standards exist for proper evaluation. Hume would himself prefer to think that the standards for writing philosophy or history ought not to be forgotten when writing poetry; equally, one ought not to forget the rhetorical demands of poetry when writing philosophy or history, in order to avoid a turgid enumeration of details.

I have elaborated upon Hume's literary achievements because they tend to be ignored or only vaguely appreciated in any discussion of his ideas. His ideas are clearly "superior" to his prose, if that kind of judgment can be made. And Hume's writings endure not because he is so compelling a figure as Dr. Johnson, but because his remarkable ideas were expressed in excellent prose. But his most important achievements lie in these fields: epistemology, ethics, history, and religion.

Hume's analysis of induction is generally regarded as his most important contribution to epistemology. Briefly, Hume argued that a sequence of events to which we have grown accustomed in the past does not logically entail that this sequence will be repeated at any future time. Or, to put it more accurately, we cannot assume that, because of the frequency of occurrence of events X belonging to class Y, that the next series of events X will also belong to class Y. Many philosophers have argued that Hume's statement of the problem is unique and that induction cannot be scientifically justified; others have argued that a "probability calculus" can be used to justify induction.[4] Bertrand Russell has observed that this form of inference (induction) "has been considered to be, like the hangman, necessary but unpleasant, and not to be talked of if the subject could possibly be avoided—except by those who, like Hume, refuse to be limited by the canons of good taste."[5] Hume's criticism of the inductive method of inference was neither recognized nor generally appreciated in his own time, with one notable exception. Speaking of the connections between cause and effect, Immanuel Kant remarked, "I openly confess, the suggestion of David Hume was the very thing, which many years ago first interrupted my dogmatic slumbers, and gave my investigations in the field of speculative philosophy quite a new direction."[6] Although Kant recognized the legitimacy of Hume's criticism of induction, he never applied his a priori theories to a solution of the problem.[7] But, since Kant's time, Hume's analysis of induction has been the subject of any number of developments, extrapolations, and refinements.

When Hume remarked in his autobiography that he considered his *Enquiry concerning the Principle of Morals* "incomparably the best" of all his writings, he simply revealed the predilection of his era for "moral science." His statement or formulation of a naturalistic ethic is often considered the most plausible yet offered,[8] and he would have appreciated the reputation it has achieved. The modern age is particularly intrigued, thanks perhaps to Wittgenstein, by Hume's discussion of the coextensiveness of ethical speculation and the structure of language. Like many other eighteenth-century writers, Hume attempted to formulate an ethic which would bridge the gap between the "dignity of human nature" and the indignities of the actions in which it all too frequently engaged. However, the reader looking for a "moral imperative" in Hume's writings will look in vain. He admits that we owe a duty to ourselves and that a concept of duty is apparent in even the "most vulgar system of morals." But Hume will not tell us "You ought to do your duty," but suggests that we will find similarities in the approbation we give to our duty to ourselves and the approbation we give to our duty to society. Individuals are uniquely responsible for their actions, and they neither should nor can expect that responsibility to be assumed by others. Man, Hume suggested, is capable of either moral strength or moral weakness, but the decision is exclusively his.

Because Hume was first a philosopher before he was a historian, the inclination is strong to draw parallels between Hume's philosophy and his judgment of events in the *History of England.* Hume's *History* is admittedly philosophical: it exhibits the judgments and discriminations we would find in good philosophical writing. But it is also a *historical* work; and its value as history cannot be overlooked. That it was widely accepted as "standard" for more than a hundred years testifies to its value as history. While the student reading Hume's *History* today might be misled about the events of English history (because of the scanty information available to Hume regarding certain eras), he would more than make up for this loss by observing Hume's mind at work in an area not always distinguished by intellectual precision. His *History of England* is not only a narrative, it is also a study of history: Hume is consciously aware of history as a process, affected by natural laws and human passions. Hume examines and discusses the ways in which these natural laws interact with human passions to produce the events of history. Thus, if we read Hume's *History* today, we can read it for information; but we can also gain from it an understanding of the process of history, not to mention certain insights into human nature as it reacts to the stress of events. And, in reading it, we will discover a very fine prose style, a quality sometimes missed in other histories of England.

History is just now beginning to lay down its judgment of Hume's contribution to religious thought. No less a thinker than Kierkegaard quoted with approval Hume's observation in "Of Miracles" that the Christian religion could not be believed without miracles and that faith was the only foundation for religion.[9] I have suggested elsewhere that Hume's initial religious skepticism was the source of his subsequent discoveries in philosophy.[10] The significance of his religious thought lies in his damaging analyses of almost all anthropomorphic conceptions of the Deity and His works. Hume so undermined the argument from design that it is no longer an intellectually respectable argument for the existence of any god. In doing so, he separated religion from epistemology and ethics and suggested that it was a discipline that would have to survive without appealing to anything but its own internal authority. To the rigidly righteous, Hume's religious thought will seem heretical. But Hume thought it equally heretical to conceive of the Deity as a species of man "writ large." To the religious inquirer, Hume's religious thought may prove to be a prolegomenon to the foundations of any true religion—faith.

Hume is, finally, what *The Times Literary Supplement* termed him, in the title to a review of Kemp Smith's edition of the *Dialogues:* an enigma.[11] Because many of his conclusions about human nature were couched in either skeptical or ironic terms, he is enigmatic. He was not a "character." He was not a stereotyped philosopher. He was, in the best eighteenth-century sense of the term, an original.

Notes and References

Chapter One

1. The complete text of this essay is reprinted in Professor Ernest Campbell Mossner's article, "David Hume's 'An Historical Essay on Chivalry and modern Honour,'" *Modern Philology*, XLV (1947), 54–60.

2. Cf. the first edition of *The History of England from the Invasion of Julius Caesar to the Accession of Henry VII* (London, 1762), I, 423. Also, *History of England* (London, 1796), II, 140–41. The passage is part of the second appendix of the discussion of the feudal and Anglo-Norman governments.

3. This is the text of that repudiation: "Most of the principles, and reasonings, contained in this volume, were published in a work in three volumes, called *A Treatise of Human Nature:* A work which the Author had projected before he left College, and which he wrote and published not long after. But not finding it successful, he was sensible of his error in going to the press too early, and he cast the whole anew in the following pieces, where some negligences in his former reasoning and more in the expression, are, he hopes, corrected. Yet several writers, who have honoured the Author's Philosophy with answers, have taken care to direct all their batteries against that juvenile work, which the Author never acknowledged, and have affected to triumph in any advantages, which, they imagined, they had obtained over it: A practice very contrary to all rules of candour and fair-dealing, and a strong instance of those polemical artifices, which a bigotted zeal thinks itself authorised to employ. Henceforth, the Author desires, that the following Pieces may alone be regarded as containing his philosophical sentiments and principles." (*Works*, III, 37–38)

4. The letter appears in *HL*, I, 12–18. John Hill Burton in his biography of Hume has identified the addressee as Dr. George Cheyne, a conjecture Greig accepts. But Professor Mossner has more convincingly identified the unknown physician as Dr. John Arbuthnot in "Hume's Epistle to Dr. Arbuthnot, 1734: The Biographical Significance," *Huntington Library Quarterly*, VII (1944), 135–52.

5. Professor Mossner's explanation and discussion of Hume's recovery is detailed and authoritative; see *Life*, pp. 81–91.

6. "Hume at La Flèche, 1735: An Unpublished Letter," ed. by E. C. Mossner, *Texas Studies in English*, XXXVII (1958), 32.

7. Cf. Alexander Pope, *Epilogue to the Satires, Dialogue II*, 226–27: "All, all but Truth, drops dead-born from the Press,/Like the last Gazette, or the last Address."

8. See E. C. Mossner's article, "The Continental Reception of Hume's *Treatise*, 1739–1741," *Mind*, LVI (1947), 31–43. The information and quotations in this paragraph about the reception of Hume's *Treatise* are from this article.

9. See the identication in *Life*, pp. 123, 618–19.

10. *An Abstract of A Treatise of Human Nature 1740, A Pamphlet hitherto unknown* by David Hume, reprinted with an Introduction by J. M. Keynes and P. Sraffa (Cambridge, 1938). For some time, biographers and scholars had thought that Adam Smith was the author of an abstract of Hume's *Treatise,* though no copy was known to exist. Keynes and Sraffa made the first discovery of the existence of the *Abstract* and conclusively identified Hume as the author. See *Life*, pp. 120–28.

11. See E. C. Mossner's essay "Hume's 'Of Criticism,'" in *Studies in Criticism and Aesthetics, 1660–1800: Essays in Honor of Samuel Holt Monk*, ed. Howard Anderson and John S. Shea (Minneapolis, 1967), pp. 232–48.

12. [David Hume], *A Letter from a Gentleman to His Friend in* Edinburgh: *containing Some Observations on A Specimen of the Principles concerning Religion and Morality,* said to be *maintain'd in a Book lately publish'd, intituled,* A Treatise of Human Nature, &c. (1745), ed. by E. C. Mossner and J. V. Price (Edinburgh, 1967). The Introduction contains a summary of events relevant to Hume's candidacy for the chair.

13. In a pamphlet generally known as *Descent on the Coast of Brittany* Hume defended General St. Clair from the ridicule of Voltaire. See Paul H. Meyer, "Voltaire and Hume's 'Descent on the Coast of Brittany,'" *Modern Language Notes*, LXVI (1951), 429–35. The pamphlet is reprinted in *Works*, IV, 443–60.

14. Conyers Middleton, *Free Enquiry into the Miraculous Powers which are supposed to have subsisted in the Christian Church from the Earliest Ages through several successive Centuries* (London, 1741).

15. C. D. Broad, *Five Types of Ethical Theory* (London, 1956), p. 9.

16. Published anonymously in London, 1749, by Andrew Millar. Skelton's biographer records that Hume was actually the reader for

the MS; see Samuel Burdy, *Life of the Late Rev. Philip Skelton* (London, 1792), pp. 99–101. Also *Life*, p. 232.

17. *Ophiomaches*, II, 42–43.

18. Several other polemicists joined the ranks of those refuting "Of Miracles." Many of them attempted to answer Hume on philosophical grounds but often found the ad hominem argument useful, e.g., "The remainder of this Essay is little more than a rude insult on the Scriptures and the *Christian* religion" (William Adams, *Essay on Mr. Hume's Essay on Miracles* [London, 1754], p. 87). Toward the conclusion of his essay, Adams inquires, "And here I ask my reader, whether he has anywhere met with either a more sceptical, disputatious turn of mind, or a more imperious, dogmatical style, than in the writings of this author?" (pp. 98–99).

Others correctly summarized Hume's position as if it represented the last outpost of nihilism or solipsism. In 1752, John Douglas, in *The Criterion: Or, Miracles Examined*, asserted that "If no event, however well attested, be credible, which contradicts experience, then there can be no certain standard of the credibility of facts . . . ," without realizing that Hume would probably agree. Douglas goes on to say that Hume's argument is sophistical because he argues that the connection between cause and effect can never be discovered. But religion is in no danger from Hume: "I shall only add, that an author who espouses such opinions [of] . . . the most extravagant scepticism . . . , can never be a dangerous enemy to religion. His arguments having novelty, may please for a while; but so opposite are they to every one's settled notions, that their influence cannot be lasting. Sorry I am to say, that the author of the *Philosophical Essays* seems to have a right to this character—a character which must sink the value of his writing, in spite of the most eminent abilities." (Quoted from a London, 1807, edition of *The Criterion*, pp. 14, 34.)

19. The first volume of Leland's *View of the Principal Deistical Writers*, which eventually ran to three volumes, was first published in 1754; the first volume paid no attention to Hume, but this oversight was rectified in a second volume of 1755. I quote from this 1755 volume; page references given in text.

20. Hume's letter is in *HL*, I, 360–61; Campbell's answer is found in the MSS of the Royal Society of Edinburgh, RSE, IV, 11, part of which is quoted in *Life*, pp. 293–94.

21. George Campbell, *A Dissertation on Miracles* (Edinburgh, 1762), pp. v–vi. Page numbers given in text hereafter.

22. The discrepancy between the date of the appearance of the *Political Discourses* given in *Works*, III, 56, and the review, which seems to appear a month earlier, is easily explained. In a letter dated Septem-

ber 29, 1751, Hume wrote to Robert Wallace: "The Discourses are at present in the Press, & will be publish'd as soon as they are printed off & sufficiently dry; which I fancy will require two or three Months" (*NHL*, p. 30). They were published by Alexander Kincaid, who also published Hume's *Essays, Moral and Political*. The reviewer for the *Monthly Review* undoubtedly used proof-sheets or early unbound copies of the *Political Discourses* for his review. The first review in the *Monthly Review* dealt with the *Enquiry concerning the Principles of Morals;* the second with the *Political Discourses* might have been published in mid-January; see *HL*, I, 167.

23. Rose's review of the second *Enquiry* appeared in *Monthly Review*, VI (January, 1752), 1–19; his review of the *Political Discourses* in the same periodical, VI (January and February, 1752), 19–43, 81–90. The passages quoted are also partially cited in *Life*, pp. 225–26.

24. The *Political Discourses* became Hume's best-known work on the Continent, translated, by itself and as part of his works, into French, German, and Italian during his lifetime. During the 1750's, the *Political Discourses* contributed to Hume's Continental reputation more than any of his other volumes. See *Life*, pp. 227–29.

25. A list of Scotticisms was prefixed to some copies of the first edition of Hume's *Political Discourses*. For Hume's correspondence with Wallace, see *NHL*, pp. 28–35.

26. Professor Eugene Rotwein has many illuminating comparisons between Hume and Smith in his edition *David Hume: Writings on Economics* (Edinburgh, 1955), *passim*. Dr. Roy Cain has written a study of Smith and Hume: "David Hume and Adam Smith: A Study in Intellectual Kinship" (Unpublished doctoral dissertation, University of Texas, 1963).

27. For the complete story of the "Conspiracy of the Booksellers," see E. C. Mossner and Harry Ransom, "Hume and the 'Conspiracy of the Booksellers': The Publication and Early Fortunes of the *History of England*," *Texas Studies in English*, XXIX (1950), 162–82.

28. *Diary of Sylas Neville, 1767–1788*, ed. Basil Cozens-Hardy (London, 1950), p. 202.

29. For the complete history of the publication of the *Four Dissertations*, see E. C. Mossner, "Hume's *Four Dissertations*: An Essay in Biography and Bibliography," *Modern Philology*, XLVIII (1950), 37–57. See also *Life*, pp. 313–35.

30. James Beattie, *Essay on Truth* (5th ed.; London, 1744), pp. 17–19.

31. Cited in *NHL*, pp. 72–73n., from a Royal Society of Edinburgh MS (III, 51).

32. Norman Kemp Smith lists only a few of the commentators who have identified Hume with Cleanthes: *Dialogues*, pp. 58–59.

33. Hayter, p. 2. Some of the other identifications of sources for the ideas in the *Dialogues* are given in Chapter 7.

34. Hayter, pp. 48–49; see *Dialogues*, p. 222.

35. See *Life*, pp. 620–22 for posthumous controversy over Hume.

Chapter Two

1. H. H. Price, "The Permanent Significance of Hume's Philosophy," *Philosophy*, XV (1940), 37.

2. Tadeusz Kozanecki, "Dawida Hume'a Niezane Listy w Zbiorach Muzeum Czartoryskich (Polska)," *Archiwum Historii Filozofii i Myśli Społecznej*, IX (1963) (*Religie Racjonalne. Studia z filozofi religii xv–xvii w*), 133.

3. Cf. Joseph Butler, Chapter I of the *Analogy of Religion* in *Works*, ed. W. E. Gladstone (Oxford, 1896), I, 29–30.

4. Norman Kemp Smith in *The Philosophy of David Hume* (London, 1949) has clearly shown that Hume's philosophy is not an adaptation of Locke and Berkeley, as was commonly thought by many commentators, among them T. H. Green in his long introduction to the *Treatise* in *Works*, I, 1–299.

5. An excellent discussion of Hume's Pyrrhonism can be found in Richard H. Popkin, "David Hume: His Pyrrhonism and his Critique of Pyrrhonism," *The Philosophical Quarterly*, I (1951), 385–407.

6. In the article mentioned in note 5 above, Professor Popkin has pointed out that Hume's formulation of Pyrrhonian skepticism differs from the standard formulation in Sextus Empiricus, and that Hume omits any reference to the methodology by which the Pyrrhonian decides practical matters once he has posited the impossibility of deciding certain questions (p. 386). Hume may be equating Pyrrhonism with the ideas attributed to Pyrrho by Pierre Bayle in his *Dictionnaire*.

7. Cf. Sextus Empiricus, *Outlines of Pyrrhonism* (London and Cambridge, 1961), I, 17; Book I, secs. 23–24.

8. In a useful article, "The Self and Perceptions: A Study in Humean Philosophy," *The Philosophical Querterly*, IX (1959), 97–115, Panayot Butcharov has argued that Hume's seeming contradiction on the concept of self is not a contradiction at all: "It amounts to the elimination of the *myself* although it preserves the existence of *selves* (as collections of perceptions)" (p. 115).

9. In the Appendix published with the third volume of the *Treatise* in 1741, Hume asserted that one could never perceive self without self having one or more perceptions and that these perceptions formed the self. See *Treatise*, Appendix, pp. 634–35.

10. This viewpoint, which I share, is Kemp Smith's, in *The Philosophy of David Hume*, pp. 160–61.

11. Kemp Smith's viewpoint "that it was through the gateway of

morals that Hume entered into his philosophy, and that, as a consequence of this, Books II and III of the *Treatise* are in date of first composition prior to the working out of the doctrines dealt with in Book I"
(p. vi) is not one I share, nor is it shared by many of Hume's other
commentators. While no one would wish to denigrate the value of
Kemp Smith's studies in Humean philosophy, I find the above assertion a little confusing when compared to his statement that "The least
original . . . part of Hume's philosophy, is his ethics" (p. 562).

12. Kemp Smith has made a useful tabulation of the passions
(p. 168); I have relied upon it somewhat for my summary.

13. Anthony Ashley Cooper, third earl of Shaftesbury is usually accounted the founder of the "Moral Sense" school. See particularly his
An Inquiry concerning VIRTUE and MERIT and *The MORALISTS;
a Philosophical Rhapsody* in *Characteristicks of Men, Manners, Opinions, Times.* For commentaries on Shaftesbury, as well as on Francis
Hutcheson and Hume, see James Bonar, *Moral Sense* (London and
New York, 1930); D. D. Raphael, *The Moral Sense* (London, 1947),
the better of the two books.

14. See A. H. Basson, *David Hume* (London, 1958), pp. 88–90.

15. John Locke, *An Essay concerning Human Understanding,* ed.
A. C. Fraser (New York, 1959), I, 142–43 (II, i, 25).

16. The most famous example of this metaphor is the Great Chain
of Being, as in Pope's *Essay on Man.* We scarcely need mention A. O.
Lovejoy's book, *The Great Chain of Being,* which is now a staple of
graduate as well as undergraduate diet.

Chapter Three

1. Hume omitted this essay from all future editions of his works,
apparently because it was "too frivolous," as he said of several others
in a letter to Adam Smith, September 24, 1752 (*HL*, I, 168).

2. See R. S. Crane's article, "Suggestions Toward a Genealogy of
the 'Man of Feeling,' " *Journal of English Literary History,* I (1934),
205–30.

3. Ralph Cohen, *The Art of Discrimination: Thomson's THE SEA-
SONS and the Language of Criticism* (Berkeley and Los Angeles,
1964).

4. The most cogent discussion of Hume's concept of taste is Ralph
Cohen's "David Hume's Experimental Method and the Theory of
Taste," *Journal of English Literary History,* XXV (1958), 270–89. I
have, in part, relied upon Professor Cohen's analysis for my understanding of both Hume's concept of taste and other eighteenth-century
uses of the term.

5. *Ibid.,* 278.

6. See Ralph Cohen, "The Transformation of Passion: A Study of

Hume's Theories of Tragedy," *Philological Quarterly*, XLI (1962), 450. Professor Cohen has provided us with the best analysis and discussion of Hume's theories of tragedy, with particular emphasis on "Of Tragedy."

7. To be discussed in the next chapter.

8. This assertion of Hume's was purely conjectural: he never married.

9. Shaftesbury's comments about Epicurus in *Miscellaneous Reflections* in Vol. III of the *Characteristicks* exemplify eighteenth-century thought in regard to Epicureanism, viz., "It need not be thought surprizing, that *Religion* it-self shou'd in the account of these Philosophers be reckon'd among those Vices and Disturbances, which it concerns us after this manner to extirpate. If the Idea of *Majesty* and *Beauty* in other inferior Subjects be in reality distracting; it must chiefly prove so, in that *principal Subject*, the Basis and Foundation of this Conceit" (*Characteristicks of Men, Manners, Opinions, Times* [Birmingham, 1773], III, 35).

10. I have discussed the irony of Hume's presentation and method in *The Ironic Hume* (Austin, Texas, 1965), pp. 22–25.

11. John Laird, *Hume's Philosophy of Human Nature* (London, 1932), p. 245.

12. Indeed, the essays contained in Hume's volume of 1752, *Political Discourses*, are primarily devoted to economic subjects. They are discussed later in this chapter.

13. See *Works*, III, 445. Also on this point, see John B. Stewart, *The Moral and Political Philosophy of David Hume* (New York, 1963), pp. 156–58.

14. This same position appears in the *History of England*, in Chapter LXXI: "And it may justly be affirmed, without any danger of exaggeration, that we, in this island, have ever since enjoyed, if not the best system of government, at least the most entire system of liberty, that ever was known amongst mankind" (*History*, VIII, 320).

15. The most recent study of Hume's treatment of mixed government in Britain is found in Stewart, pp. 221–55.

16. Laird, p. 257.

17. See Eugene Rotwein, *David Hume: Writings on Economics* (Edinburgh, 1955), p. xxxii. Professor Rotwein's discussion of Hume's economic thought is exemplary, and I have relied on it to some extent for my discussion here.

18. See Rotwein, p. lv.

19. *Ibid.*, pp. liv–lvii.

Chapter Four

1. Selby-Bigge's editions of Hume's *Treatise* and *Enquiries* are standard, which is deplorable. While the *Treatise* is relatively free of errors, it has not really been edited; and the omissions and distortions in the first *Enquiry* have made it almost useless as a text for the study of Hume's philosophy. The Clarendon Press, apprised of the defects of Selby-Bigge's editions, is planning to publish a new edition of Hume's philosophical works.

2. This attitude is adopted for a cogent book on Hume by Antony Flew, *Hume's Philosophy of Belief* (London, 1961). My discussion in this chapter owes much to Professor Flew's arguments and insights; his book is by all odds the best work done on Hume's first *Enquiry*. Too, I ought to remind the reader here that the *Enquiry concerning Human Understanding* acquired that title only in the 1758 edition of the *Essays and Treatises on Several Subjects;* it was originally published in 1748 as *Philosophical Essays concerning Human Understanding.*

3. This quotation acts as subtitle and unifying theme in Professor Mossner's *Life.* The idea permeates all of Hume's writings, from the political essays to the *History of England* and must be a part of any evaluation of Hume's philosophy. See, for example, Flew, p. 9.

4. This method of inquiry apparently has always been popular with philosophers, and Hume records in his letters his questions to the blind poet Blacklock (*HL,* I, 201, 209) that Blacklock could form no idea of color but that he formed certain associations with words whose origin in perception was unknown to him.

5. "Of Miracles" and "Of a Particular Providence and a Future State," Sections X and XI respectively, constitute more of an appendix than anything else—but they are nonetheless the most devastating part of the *Enquiry.*

6. Flew, p. 53.

7. Cf. Flew, pp. 108–9. Flew has described the methodology for Hume's approach to the problems of causality and necessary connection as "psychogenetic."

8. The reader who is interested in a more extensive discussion of Section VIII can consult Flew, pp. 140–65.

9. Bertrand Russell, *Why I Am Not a Christian* (New York, 1957), p. v.

10. See A. E. Taylor, *David Hume and the Miraculous* (Cambridge, 1927), pp. 53–54.

11. Cf. *HL,* I, 154: "What Danger can ever come from ingenious Reasoning & Enquiry?"

12. Isaac Newton, *Optics,* III, i, 31; cf. Flew, p. 269.

13. See Flew, pp. 271–72.

14. These ideas are found in a passage omitted in the authorized editions of Hume's works published after 1760; cf. *Works,* IV, 173n. Yet the same import of the ideas remains in the *Enquiry concerning the Principles of Morals.*

15. Hume's use of the concept of self-love is only one of very many in the Restoration and eighteenth century; the term is peculiarly associated with eighteenth-century thought (see James Hastings, *Encyclopædia of Religion and Ethics* [Edinburgh, 1958], XI, 359).

16. Many of Butler's sermons are concerned with the difficulties of reconciling the seemingly opposite qualities of benevolence and self-love. See his *Works,* ed. by The Right Hon. W. E. Gladstone (Oxford, 1896), II, 21–28; 185–228.

17. This is not Hume's example but an extrapolation. Hume apparently had some second thoughts about the principle of universality in discourses about ethics. Cf. *A Dialogue* published along with the first edition of the *Enquiry concerning the Principles of Morals;* there Hume outlines some ideas in antiquity which would cause revulsion or disapproval in eighteenth-century man but which were acceptable and even praiseworthy in antiquity.

Chapter Five

1. See E. C. Mossner, "An Apology for David Hume, Historian," *Publications of the Modern Language Association,* LVI (1941), 675–76, for a list of the manuscript sources testifying to Hume's early interest in and plans for writing a history of England. Mossner thoroughly demolishes the once-popular notion that Hume's *History* was neither scholarly nor careful. Hume had at his command useful and sometimes unique resources, and he used them painstakingly.

2. Manuscript notes for the *History of England* are now in the archives of the National Library of Scotland (MSS 733–34) and the Huntington Library in San Marino, California (MS HM 12263). See *Life,* p. 301.

3. Ralph's work may also be exhaustive, but I have been able to read only part of its two volumes. Each volume is about the size of a demy folio, contains over a thousand pages, and is elaborately annotated.

4. [James Ralph], *The History of England: during the Reigns of K. William, Q. Anne, and K. George I., with an Introductory Review of the Reigns of the Royal Brothers, Charles and James; in which are to be found the Seeds of the Revolution* (London, 1744), I, 1. Ralph published the work anonymously; the title-page lists the work *By a Lover of Truth and Liberty.*

5. Ralph, I, 1.

6. Fraser was an acquaintance of Hume, who parodied his rabid Jacobitism in a pamphlet, never published, entitled *To the Right Honble the Lord-Chief-Justice Reason, and the Honble the Judges, Discretion, Prudence, Reserve, and Deliberation, The Petition of the Patients of Westminster against James Fraser, apothecary*. Printed in *HL*, II, 340–42. Cf. *HL*, I, 146–48.

7. Section II of this chapter will contain an inquiry into Hume's *History* as a philosophical work.

8. John Bennet Black, *The Art of History* (London, 1926), p. 85.

9. Black, p. 90.

10. In 1773, Dr. Johnson had not yet read Hume's *History*. See James Boswell, *Life of Johnson*, ed. Hill and Powell (Oxford, 1934–50), II, 236–37.

11. W. E. H. Lecky, *A History of England in the Eighteenth Century* (London, 1925), I, 329–30. For a thorough discussion of the Naturalisation Bill, see Cecil Roth, *A History of the Jews in England* (Oxford, 1949), pp. 215–21.

12. For Hume's sympathetic attitude, if a bit tinged with irony, towards Jews, see *HL*, I, 423–24.

13. I have discussed Hume's concept of civil and individual liberty in "Hume's Concept of Liberty and *The History of England*," *Studies in Romanticism*, V (1966), 139–57.

14. See his column for October 22, 1964, "Nonsense about Anti-Intellectualism."

Chapter Six

1. When *Four Dissertations*, containing "The Natural History of Religion," appeared in February, 1747, Warburton made good his earlier threat to publish a "refutation" of Hume; accordingly, he published the work described in the following note. For additional information, see *Life*, p. 326.

2. *A Selection from Unpublished Papers of the Right Reverend William Warburton*, ed. Francis Kilvert (London, 1841), pp. 309–10. Warburton published a reply to "The Natural History of Religion," under circumstances which made clear that he did not want to be identified as the author. Warburton's tract was called *Remarks on Mr. David Hume's Essay on the Natural History of Religion: Addressed to the Rev. Dr. Warburton* (London, 1757). The book was actually a culling of marginal remarks in his copy of Hume's essay. Writing to Richard Hurd in early 1757, Warburton said the reply should "bear something like this title, *Remarks on Mr. Hume's late Essay, called the Natural History of Religion, by a Gentleman of Cambridge, in a Letter to the Rev. Dr. W*. I propose the address should be with the dryness and reserve of a stranger, who likes the method of the Letters on

Bolingbroke's Philosophy, and follows it here against the same sort of writer, inculcating the same impiety, naturalism, and employing the same kind of arguments. The address will remove it from me: the author, a *Gentleman of Cambridge,* from you; and the secrecy in printing from us both." (*Letters from a Late Eminent Prelate to One of his Friends* [2nd ed.; London, 1809], p. 241.) Why Warburton, who had never been shy about his "triumphs" over skepticism, should want to publish this work in secrecy is a mystery. The abusiveness of the contents may be the reason.

3. *Works,* IV, 309. A separate edition of "The Natural History of Religion," ed. H. E. Root (London, 1956), with an informative introduction is available. Hereafter, I give references in text, with a cross-reference to Root's edition.

4. E. C. Mossner in "The Enigma of Hume," *Mind,* XIV (1936), 334–49 makes the estimate based on the page count given in J. Y. T. Greig's *David Hume* (London, 1931), p. 236 and n.

5. For a discussion of Hume's irony in general, see my *The Ironic Hume.* Chapter 4 contains an analysis of the irony in the *Dialogues.*

6. See my two articles, "Empirical Theists in Cicero and Hume," *Texas Studies in Literature and Language,* V (1963), 255–64, and "Sceptics in Cicero and Hume," *Journal of the History of Ideas,* XXV (1964), 97–106.

7. Cicero, *De Natura Deorum,* trans. H. Rackham (Cambridge, 1956), p. 383.

8. Mossner, "The Enigma of Hume," pp. 314–47.

9. See R. H. Hurlbutt III, "David Hume and Scientific Theism," *Journal of the History of Ideas,* XVII (1956), 493–96.

10. Preserved Smith, *A History of Modern Culture* (New York, 1962), II, 448.

11. C. W. Hendel, *Studies in the Philosophy of David Hume* (New York, 1963), p. 278.

12. See Kemp Smith's list in *Dialogues,* pp. 58–59 and n.

13. Milner, *op. cit.,* p. 221.

14. Mossner, "The Enigma of Hume," p. 336.

15. Preserved Smith, II, 448.

16. Hendel, p. 278.

17. Preserved Smith, II, 448.

18. John Hill Burton, *Life and Correspondence of David Hume* (Edinburgh, 1846), I, 328, 330.

19. Hendel, p. 278.

20. Cf. Mossner, "The Enigma of Hume," p. 334; also Kemp Smith's Introduction to *Dialogues* and pp. 59–75.

21. Hendel, pp. 271–72.

22. This passage is a footnote to a paragraph Hume added in the

appendix affixed to Vol. III of the first ed. of the *Treatise*. See *Treatise*, I, iii, 14; also *Works*, I,455–56 and n.

23. Cf. *Dialogues*, pp. 132–33 and *Treatise*, I, iv, 7.

24. Compare Pope, *Essay on Man*, III, 7–14:
Look round our World; behold the chain of Love
Combining all below and all above.
See plastic Nature working to this end,
The single atoms each to other tend,
Attract, attracted to, the next in place
Form'd and impell'd its neighbour to embrace.
See Matter next, with various life endu'd,
Press to one centre still, the gen'ral Good.

25. For a typically modern analysis of the moral problem of evil discussed in Parts X and XI of the *Dialogues*, see Nelson Pike, "Hume on Evil," *The Philosophical Review*, LXXII (1963), 180–97. I must confess that I am not quite sure what Professor Pike has done in this article, but his purpose was to disentangle the various observations Hume makes about evil in those two books of the *Dialogues*.

Chapter Seven

1. René Wellek, Review of *The Forgotten Hume*, *Philological Quarterly*, XXIII (1944), 169; the italics are Wellek's.

2. See the two books by Professor W. K. Wimsatt, Jr., on Johnson's prose style, *The Prose Style of Samuel Johnson* (New Haven and London, 1941), Chapter 8; also *Philosophic Words: A Study of Style and Meaning in the "Rambler" and "Dictionary" of Samuel Johnson* (New Haven, 1948).

3. In his *Life and Correspondence of David Hume* (Edinburgh, 1846) John Hill Burton prints (I, 228–231) some poems in Hume's handwriting from manuscripts in the Royal Society of Edinburgh. They are undoubtedly Hume's, but he does not mention them in his letters, and of course, they were never published.

4. See Hans Reichenbach, *The Theory of Probability* (Berkeley and Los Angeles, 1949), pp. vii–ix, 469–82.

5. *Human Knowledge: Its Scope and Limits* (London, 1956), p. 451.

6. *Prolegomena to any Future Metaphysics*, ed. by Paul Carus (Chicago, 1949), p. 7.

7. This circumstance led Bertrand Russell to remark, "After meditating for twelve years, he produced his great work, the *Critique of Pure Reason;* seven years later, at the age of sixty-four, he produced the *Critique of Practical Reason*, in which he resumed his dogmatic slumbers after nearly twenty years of uncomfortable wakefulness." *Unpopular Essays* (New York, 1950), p. 51.

8. H. H. Price, *op. cit.*, p. 36.

9. Walter Lowrie, *A Short Life of Kierkegaard* (Princeton, 1942), p. 108.

10. *The Ironic Hume*, pp. 146–52.

11. See the issue for November 2, 1935; also E. C. Mossner's article with the same title, "The Enigma of Hume."

Selected Bibliography

PRIMARY SOURCES

The following texts were consulted for quotations from Hume's writings. Those marked with * are standard editions.

*An Abstract of a Treatise of Human Nature (1740): A Pamphlet hitherto unknown by David Hume. Reprinted with introduction by J. M. KEYNES and P. SRAFFA. Cambridge: The University Press, 1938. (Cited as Abstract.)

*Dialogues concerning Natural Religion, ed. by NORMAN KEMP SMITH. New York: Social Sciences Publishers, 1948. Reprinted in Library of Liberal Arts series, 1964. (Cited as Dialogues.)

An Enquiry concerning Human Understanding, ed. by E. C. MOSSNER. New York: Washington Square Press, 1963. (A reprint of the second edition, published in London, 1750. Cited as ECHU.)

An Inquiry concerning the Principles of Morals, ed. by C. W. HENDEL. New York: Liberal Arts Press, 1957. (Cited as ECPM.)

The History of England, from the Invasion of Julius Caesar to the Revolution in 1688. 8 vols. London: T. Cadell, 1796. (Cited as History.)

*The Letters of David Hume, ed. by J. Y. T. GREIG. 2 vols. Oxford: The Clarendon Press, 1932. (Cited as HL.)

*New Letters of David Hume, ed. by RAYMOND KLIBANSKY and E. C. MOSSNER. Oxford: The Clarendon Press, 1954. (Cited as NHL.)

*The Philosophical Works of David Hume, ed. by T. H. GREEN and T. H. GROSE. 4 vols. London: Longmans, Green, and Co., 1874–75. (Contains all of Hume's works, except the History, the Bellmen's Petition, and the Account of Stewart. Cited as Works.)

*A Treatise of Human Nature, ed. by L. A. SELBY-BIGGE. Oxford: The Clarendon Press, 1955. (Cited as Treatise.)

SECONDARY SOURCES

The following items may be consulted for more detailed commentaries on Hume's life and writings.

BASSON, A. H. David Hume. London: Penguin Books, 1958. Introductory book, devoted mostly to Hume's principles of knowledge, morality, and religion.

BECKER, CARL L. *The Heavenly City of the Eighteenth-Century Philosophers.* New Haven: Yale University Press, 1960. Contains some interesting misunderstandings of Hume.

BRUNIUS, TEDDY. *David Hume on Criticism.* (Figura: Studies edited by the Institute of Art History, University of Uppsala, No. 2) Stockholm: Almqvist and Wiksell, 1952. Only book-length study of Hume's critical principles, not a very successful one at that.

COHEN, RALPH. "David Hume's Experimental Method and the Theory of Taste," *Journal of English Literary History,* XXV (1958), 270–89. Thorough and penetrating analysis of Hume's concept of taste; valuable historical information.

———. "The Transformation of Passion: A Study of Hume's Theories of Tragedy," *Philological Quarterly,* XLI (1962), 450–64. Excellent study of the development of Hume's theories of tragedy.

——— (ed.). *Essential Works of David Hume.* New York: 1965. Useful and inexpensive paperback selection of Hume's works, including complete texts of *An Enquiry concerning Human Understanding, An Enquiry concerning the Principles of Morals,* the *Dialogues concerning Natural Religion,* various essays, and the *Abstract.*

FLEW, ANTONY. *Hume's Philosophy of Belief: A Study of his First Inquiry.* London: Routledge and Kegan Paul; New York: Humanities Press, 1961. Devoted exclusively to the *Enquiry concerning Human Understanding;* very useful.

HENDEL, CHARLES WILLIAM, JR. *Studies in the Philosophy of David Hume.* New York: Liberal Arts Press, 1963. Contains a review of Hume scholarship since 1925, mostly concerned interpretations of Hume by various modern philosophers.

HORN, DAVID B. "Hume as Historian" in *University of Edinburgh 250th Anniversary of the Birth of David Hume (1711:1961) A Record of the Commemoration Published as a Supplement to the University Gazette.* Edinburgh: The University Press, 1961. Pp. 25–28. Good appraisal of Hume's value as historian.

HUXLEY, THOMAS H. *Hume, With Helps to the Study of Berkeley.* New York: Appleton, 1897. Great agnostic writes about great skeptic, with some interesting results.

JESSOP, T. E. *A Bibliography of David Hume and of Scottish Philosophy from Francis Hutcheson to Lord Balfour.* London: A. Brown & Sons, 1938. New edition forthcoming.

LAIRD, JOHN. *Hume's Philosophy of Human Nature.* London: Methuen and Co., 1932. Good general study of Hume's philosophy.

LEROY, ANDRE. *La Critique et la Religion chez David Hume.* Paris: F. Alcan, 1930. Lengthy study of Hume's religious thought.

McGILVARY, E. B. "Altruism in Hume's *Treatise,*" *Philosophical Review,* XII (1903), 272–98. Argues that Hume admits the existence of an original altruism in the *Treatise.*

MACNABB, D. G. C. *David Hume: His Theory of Knowledge and Morality.* London: Hutchinson's University Library, 1951. Contains useful exegeses of Hume's theories of the understanding.

MOSSNER, ERNEST CAMPBELL. "An Apology for David Hume, Historian," *PMLA,* LVI (1941), 657–90. Valuable information about the composition and structure of the *History.*

———. "The Enigma of Hume," *Mind,* XIV (1936), 334–49. Concerned with the identity of the participants in the *Dialogues.*

———. *The Forgotten Hume: Le bon David.* New York: Columbia University Press, 1943. Discusses Hume's relations with various eighteenth-century literary figures.

———. *The Life of David Hume.* Austin: The University of Texas Press; London and Edinburgh: Thomas Nelson and Sons, Ltd., 1954. The standard biography, not likely to be excelled. (Cited as *Life.*)

——— (ed.). "New Hume Letters to Lord Elibank," *Texas Studies in Literature and Language,* IV (1962), 431–60. Additional Hume letters.

NORTON, DAVID FATE and POPKIN, RICHARD H. (eds.). *David Hume: Philosophical Historian.* New York: The Library of Liberal Arts (The Bobbs-Merrill Company, Inc.), 1965. Selection from Hume's works of items bearing on his position as a historian; Professor Norton has contributed an essay on "History and Philosophy in Hume's Thought" and Professor Popkin on "Skepticism and the Study of History."

POPKIN, RICHARD H. "David Hume: his Pyrrhonism and his Critique of Pyrrhonism," *Philosophical Quarterly,* I (1951), 385–407. Excellent commentary on Hume's Pyrrhonistic skepticism.

PRICE, H. H. "The Permanent Significance of Hume's Philosophy," *Philosophy,* XV (1940), 7–37. Sensible appraisal of the value of Hume's contributions to philosophical discourse.

PRICE, J. V. *The Ironic Hume.* Austin: The University of Texas Press, 1965. Study of the ironic structure of Hume's language and thought; reprints Hume's *Bellmen's Petition* and *Account of Stewart.*

ROTWEIN, EUGENE. *David Hume: Writings on Economics.* Edinburgh: Thomas Nelson and Sons, Ltd., 1955. Reprints Hume's economic essays with elaborate introduction and commentary.

SMITH, NORMAN KEMP. *The Philosophy of David Hume: A Critical Study of Its Origins and Central Doctrines.* London: Macmillan and Co., 1949. Best general study of Hume's philosophy, detailed and authoritative.

STEWART, JOHN B. *The Moral and Political Philosophy of David Hume.* New York and London: Columbia University Press, 1963. Excellent and valuable discussion, superior in many ways to Kemp Smith's.

Index